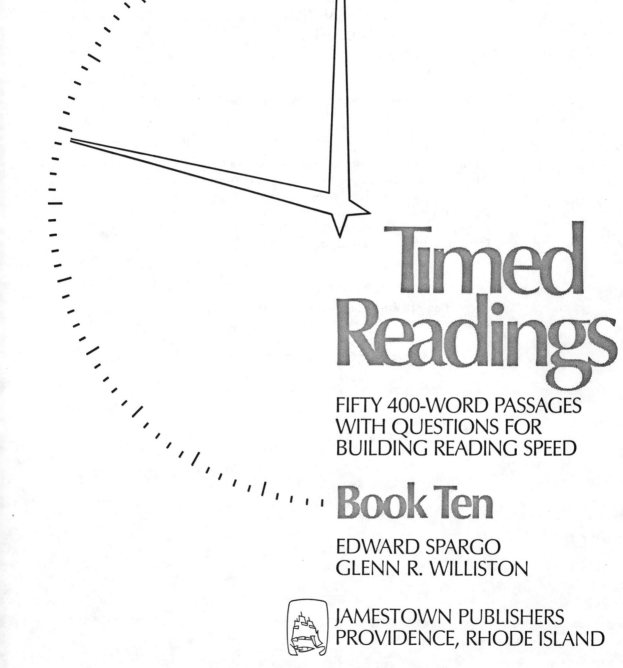

Timed Readings

FIFTY 400-WORD PASSAGES
WITH QUESTIONS FOR
BUILDING READING SPEED

Book Ten

EDWARD SPARGO
GLENN R. WILLISTON

JAMESTOWN PUBLISHERS
PROVIDENCE, RHODE ISLAND

TIMED READINGS
No. 810, Book 10

Cover Design by Stephen R. Anthony

Illustrations by Mari-Ann Süvari

Printed in the United States
KI 84 85 86 9 8 7 6 5

ISBN 0-89061-038-X

Contents

To the Instructor

Timed Readings is designed to provide plentiful practice in building reading speed—and comprehension—using graded selections of standard word length.

The Reading Selections

For any drill to be productive and meaningful, all the elements of the practice, except the one being taught, should be held constant. In *Timed Readings* the selections in all ten books are 400 words long and all deal with factual information.

The variable element in the series is the reading level of the selections. Starting at grade four, each book advances one grade level, ending at college level. Readability of the selections was assessed by applying Fry's *Formula for Assessing Readability*, using two samples from each selection.

Placement in the Series

To become faster and better readers using *Timed Readings,* students must start at a suitable reading level. For speed practice this means one or two levels below the student's instructional level. For most average readers, a suitable level would probably be a reading level one or two grades below their present grade in school.

How Fast Is Fast?

What is the optimum rate for each reader? Only individual students can determine the limits to which they can be challenged. Just as timing elicits exceptional performance from the athlete, the irrepressible impulse of the reader to beat the clock can produce spectacular progress.

For many students a rate of 400 words a minute would be impressive, if sustained, on factual material of the type included in *Timed Readings.* However, this rate should not be imposed as a standard for everyone, nor should it be allowed to become a ceiling for talented students.

Timing the Selections

To help students time the selections, this method is suggested. Write on the blackboard these times:

:10	:20	:30	:40	:50	1:00
1:10	1:20	1:30	1:40	1:50	2:00
2:10	2:20	2:30	2:40	2:50	3:00
3:10	3:20	3:30	3:40	3:50	4:00
4:10	4:20	4:30	4:40	4:50	5:00

Give students the signal to preview. Allow 30 seconds for this.

Direct students to read the selection and begin timing. At the end of ten seconds, erase *:10;* ten seconds later, erase *:20;* ten seconds later, erase *:30,* and so on until all the numbers have been erased or all the students have finished reading.

Instruct students to look up to the board when they finish reading and copy the lowest time remaining—the next number to be erased. This is their reading time. This number should be written on the top line *(Reading Time)* in the timing box at the top of the page they have just read.

Scheduling the Pacing Drills

A feature of the revised edition of *Timed Readings* is the opportunity to offer pacing drills. Page 9 describes these drills and the value of them. A section addressed to the instructor discusses how and when the drills may be scheduled and how to set the pace for the drills.

The Comprehension Questions

No achiever can claim success until he or she has been tested. In the case of *Timed Readings,* speed without comprehension is meaningless. Students must display adequate comprehension before their rate can be considered valid. Comprehension scores of 70 to 80 percent indicate that learners are properly placed within the series and are comprehending satisfactorily.

The questions accompanying the selections were constructed with a single purpose in mind—to demonstrate that the reader has, in fact, read the selection. In this regard, the questions may be considered comprehension checks rather than comprehension tests. A mix of question types—five fact and five thought questions—accompanies each selection.

An answer key on pages 116 and 117 permits immediate correction of responses and reinforcement of learning.

The Progress Graph

Industry has discovered the usefulness of charts and graphs for employee motivation. The graphs on pages 118 and 119 help students visualize their progress and reinforce their incentive to progress even further. Encourage students to maintain comprehension scores of 70 to 80 percent while gradually increasing their reading rate.

The legend on the right-hand side of the progress graphs automatically converts reading times into words-per-minute reading rates.

Another graph is provided on page 120 for students to use to plot their success with the pacing drills.

Advancement to Successive Levels

A student who has reached a peak of reading speed (with satisfactory comprehension) is ready to advance to the next book in the *Timed Readings* series. For example, a student who consistently achieves a reading rate of 400 words per minute with 80 percent or higher comprehension might better be challenged to transfer this achievement to a higher and more difficult level in the series. However, students should be encouraged to maintain their rate on a number of selections in order to consolidate their achievement before moving on to the higher level.

How to Use This Book

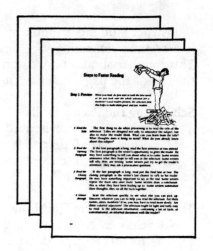

1. Learn the Four Steps. Study and learn the four steps to follow to become a better and faster reader. The steps are covered on pages 10, 11, 12 and 13.

2. Find Reading Selection. Turn to the selection you are going to read and wait for the instructor's signal to preview. Your instructor will allow 30 seconds for previewing.

3. Begin Reading. When your instructor gives you the signal, begin reading. Read at a slightly faster-than-normal speed. Read well enough so that you will be able to answer questions about what you have read.

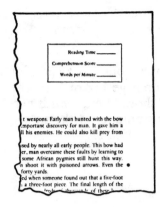

4. Fill in Timing Box. When you finish reading, look at the blackboard and note your reading time. Your reading time will be the lowest time remaining on the board, or the next number to be erased. Write this time in the timing box at the top of the page on the first line, *Reading Time.*

5. Answer Questions. Turn the page and answer the ten questions on the back. There are five fact questions and five thought questions. Pick the *best* answer to each question and put an *x* in that box.

6. Correct Your Answers. Using the Answer Key on pages 116 and 117, correct your work. Circle your wrong answers and put an *x* in the box you should have marked. Score 10 points for each correct answer. Write your score in the timing box on the second line, *Comprehension Score.*

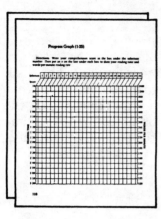

7. Fill in Progress Graph. Enter your score and plot your reading time on the graph on page 118 or 119. The right-hand side of the graph shows your words-per-minute reading speed. Write this number in the timing box on the bottom line, *Words per Minute.*

Instructions for the Pacing Drills

From time to time your instructor may wish to conduct pacing drills using *Timed Readings.* For this work you need to use the Pacing Dots printed in the margins of your book pages. These dots will help you regulate your reading speed to match the pace set by your instructor or announced on the cassette tape.

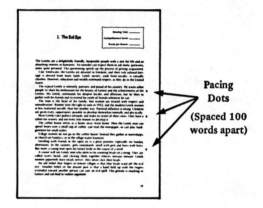

Pacing Dots

(Spaced 100 words apart)

You will be reading at the correct pace if you are at the dot when your instructor says "Mark" or when you hear the tone on the tape. If you are ahead of the pace, read a little more slowly; if you are behind the pace, increase your reading speed. Try to match the pace exactly.

Follow these steps.

Step 1: Record the Pace. In the timing box at the top of the page, write on the line labeled *Words per Minute* the rate announced by the instructor or by the speaker on the tape.

Step 2: Begin Reading. Wait for the signal to begin reading. Read at a slightly faster-than-normal speed. You will not know how on-target your pace is until you hear your instructor say "Mark" or you hear the first tone on the tape. After a little practice you will be able to select an appropriate starting speed most of the time.

Step 3: Adjust Your Pace. As you read, try to match the pace set by the instructor or the tape. Read more slowly or more quickly as necessary. You should be reading the line beside a dot when you hear the pacing signal. The pacing sounds may distract you at first. Don't worry about it. Keep reading and your concentration will return.

Step 4: Stop and Answer Questions. Stop reading when you are told to, even if you have not finished the selection. Answer the questions right away. Correct your work and record your score in the timing box on the second line, *Comprehension Score*. Strive to maintain 80 percent comprehension on each drill as you gradually increase your pace.

Step 5: Fill in the Pacing Graph. Transfer your words-per-minute rate to the box labeled *Pace* on the pacing graph on page 120. Then plot your comprehension score on the line beneath the box.

These pacing drills are designed to help you become a more flexible reader. They encourage you to "break out" of a pattern of reading everything at the same speed.

The drills help in other ways, too. Sometimes in a reading program you reach a certain level and bog down. You don't seem able to move on and progress. These pacing drills will help you to work your way out of such slumps and get your reading program moving again.

To the Instructor

As a variation in the *Timed Readings* routine, try to schedule pacing drills at least once a week. Select an appropriate starting pace, one that is comfortable for everyone in the class. Do four or five drills, increasing the pace each time.

A Pacing Cassette is available which directs students through the drills. If you are not using the cassette, follow the guide at right to set the pace.

To set a pace of	
100 wpm, say "Mark" every	60 seconds
125	48
150	40
175	34
200	30
225	26
250	24
275	22
300	20
325	18
350	17
375	16
400	15
425	14
450	13
500	12
550	11
600	10
650	9
750	8
850	7
1000	6

Steps to Faster Reading

Step 1: Preview *When you read, do you start in with the first word, or do you look over the whole selection for a moment? Good readers preview the selection first— this helps to make them good, and fast, readers.*

1. Read the Title

The first thing to do when previewing is to read the title of the selection. Titles are designed not only to announce the subject, but also to make the reader think. What can you learn from the title? What thoughts does it bring to mind? What do you already know about this subject?

2. Read the Opening Paragraph

If the first paragraph is long, read the first sentence or two instead. The first paragraph is the writer's opportunity to greet the reader. He may have something to tell you about what is to come. Some writers announce what they hope to tell you in the selection. Some writers tell why they are writing. Some writers just try to get the reader's attention—they may ask a provocative question.

3. Read the Closing Paragraph

If the last paragraph is long, read just the final line or two. The closing paragraph is the writer's last chance to talk to his reader. He may have something important to say at the end. Some writers repeat the main idea once more. Some writers draw a conclusion: this is what they have been leading up to. Some writers summarize their thoughts; they tie all the facts together.

4. Glance through

Scan the selection quickly to see what else you can pick up. Discover whatever you can to help you read the selection. Are there names, dates, numbers? If so, you may have to read more slowly. Are there colorful adjectives? The selection might be light and fairly easy to read. Is the selection informative, containing a lot of facts, or conversational, an informal discussion with the reader?

Steps to Faster Reading

Step 2:
Read for Meaning

When you read, do you just see words? Are you so occupied reading words that you sometimes fail to get the meaning? Good readers see beyond the words—they read for meaning. This makes them faster readers.

1. Build Concentration

You cannot read with understanding if you are not concentrating. Every reader's mind wanders occasionally; it is not a cause for alarm. When you discover that your thoughts have strayed, correct the situation right away. The longer you wait, the harder it becomes. Avoid distractions and distracting situations. Outside noises and activities will compete for your attention if you let them. Keep the preview information in mind as you read. This will help to focus your attention on the selection.

2. Read in Thought Groups

Individual words do not tell us much. They must be combined with other words in order to yield meaning. To obtain meaning from the printed page, therefore, the reader should see the words in meaningful combinations. If you see only a word at a time (called word-by word reading), your comprehension suffers along with your speed. To improve both speed and comprehension, try to group the words into phrases which have a natural relationship to each other. For practice, you might want to read aloud, trying to speak the words in meaningful combinations.

3. Question the Author

To sustain the pace you have set for yourself, and to maintain a high level of comprehension, question the writer as you read. Continually ask yourself such questions as, "What does this mean? What is he saying now? How can I use this information?" Questions like these help you to concentrate fully on the selection.

Steps to Faster Reading

Step 3:
Grasp Paragraph Sense

The paragraph is the basic unit of meaning. If you can discover quickly and understand the main point of each paragraph, you can comprehend the author's message. Good readers know how to find the main ideas of paragraphs quickly. This helps to make them faster readers.

DISCOVERING THE MAIN POINT

1. Find the Topic Sentence

The topic sentence, the sentence containing the main idea, is often the first sentence of a paragraph. It is followed by other sentences which support, develop, or explain the main idea. Sometimes a topic sentence comes at the end of a paragraph. When it does, the supporting details come first, building the base for the topic sentence. Some paragraphs do not have a topic sentence. Such paragraphs usually create a mood or feeling, rather than present information.

2. Understand Paragraph Structure

Every well-written paragraph has purpose. The purpose may be to inform, define, explain, persuade, compare or contrast, illustrate, and so on. The purpose should always relate to the main idea and expand on it. As you read each paragraph, see how the body of the paragraph is used to tell you more about the main idea or topic sentence. Read the supporting details intelligently, recognizing that what you are reading is all designed to develop the single main idea.

Steps to Faster Reading

Step 4: Organize Facts

When you read, do you tend to see a lot of facts without any apparent connection or relationship? Understanding how the facts all fit together to deliver the author's message is, after all, the reason for reading. Good readers organize facts as they read. This helps them to read rapidly and well.

1. Discover the Writer's Plan

Look for a clue or signal word early in the article which might reveal the author's structure. Every writer has a plan or outline which he follows. If the reader can discover his method of organization, he has the key to understanding the message. Sometimes the author gives you obvious signals. If he says, "There are three reasons . . ." the wise reader looks for a listing of the three items. Other less obvious signal words such as *moreover, otherwise, consequently* all tell the reader the direction the writer's message will take.

2. Relate as You Read

As you read the selection, keep the information learned during the preview in mind. See how the ideas you are reading all fit into place. Consciously strive to relate what you are reading to the title. See how the author is carrying through in his attempt to piece together a meaningful message. As you discover the relationship among the ideas, the message comes through quickly and clearly.

1. The Evil Eye

Reading Time _____

Comprehension Score _____

Words per Minute _____

The Greeks are a delightfully friendly, hospitable people with a zest for life and an absorbing interest in humanity. An outsider can expect them to ask many questions, some quite personal. This questioning speeds up the process of getting acquainted.

Like Americans, the Greeks are devoted to freedom, and their rich cultural heritage is derived from many lands. Greek society, aside from royalty, is virtually classless. However, education and wealth command respect, as they do in the United States.

The typical Greek is intensely patriotic and proud of his country. He wants other people to share his enthusiasm for the beauty of Greece and the achievements of the Greeks. His family commands his deepest loyalty and affection, but he likes to gather with his friends and to extend his circle of friends whenever he can.

The man is the head of his family, but women are treated with respect and consideration. Women won the right to vote in 1952, and the modern Greek woman is less restricted socially than her mother was. Parental influence is strong. Children are given every opportunity possible to develop themselves mentally and physically.

Most Greeks take politics seriously and make no secret of their views. They have a talent for oratory and use every free minute to develop it.

The coffee house serves as a home away from home. Here the Greek man can spend hours over a small cup of coffee, can read the newspaper, or can play backgammon for small stakes.

Village women do not go to the coffee house. Instead they gather at sweetshops, at church on Sundays, or at the village water fountain.

Strolling with friends in the open air is a great pastime, especially on Sunday afternoons. In the country, girls customarily stroll with girls and boys with boys. But many a young man spots his future bride in the course of a stroll.

A visitor will see Greek men who seem to be counting beads on a string. They are called worry beads, and clicking them together relieves nervous tension. Greek women apparently have steady nerves—they never click their beads.

An old belief that lingers in remote villages is that blue beads ward off the evil eye. Another belief of the distant past is that a hand held up with the fingers extended toward another person can cast an evil spell. This gesture is insulting in Greece and can lead to violent argument.

15

Selection 1: Recalling Facts

1. Like Americans, the Greeks are devoted to
   □ a. faithfulness.   □ b. freedom.   □ c. friendship.

2. Greek women won the right to vote in the early
   □ a. 1940s.   □ b. 1950s.   □ c. 1960s.

3. Many Greeks have a talent for
   □ a. painting.   □ b. oratory.   □ c. writing.

4. In the coffee houses, Greek men enjoy playing
   □ a. backgammon.   □ b. chess.   □ c. parcheesi.

5. The favorite pastime on Sunday afternoons in Greece is
   □ a. visiting friends. □ b. walking.   □ c. meeting at sweetshops.

Selection 1: Understanding Ideas

6. The author implies that
   □ a. Greeks talk at great lengths about politics.
   □ b. Greeks are often suspicious of strangers.
   □ c. Greeks like to travel.

7. Visitors to Greece often find that natives are
   □ a. energetic.   □ b. inquisitive.   □ c. quiet.

8. Greek men can be seen clicking beads
   □ a. when they are worrying.
   □ b. when they are praying.
   □ c. when they are counting.

9. In some Greek villages
   □ a. women have no rights.
   □ b. old men are revered.
   □ c. people are superstitious.

10. The reader can conclude that
    □ a. Greece is a land of striking contrasts.
    □ b. Greece is a land of strange and unusual sights.
    □ c. Greece is a land of warmth and vitality.

2. Cats' Eyes

Reading Time _____

Comprehension Score _____

Words per Minute _____

What do cats' eyes and highway reflector signs have in common? They both act as retroreflectors.

Almost everyone has noticed the eerie, frightening appearance of animals at night, as their eyes seem to glow in reflected light. One may speculate that just as reflective highway signs alert the motorist to many road hazards, so early man was often warned of danger by light from his campfire reflected in the eyes of lurking predators. In both cases, the light is retroreflected, giving it a particularly bright appearance.

The principles of retroreflection have been understood for centuries. However, it is only within the last fifty or sixty years, with the wide use of the automobile, that this area of optics has received important commercial application. Today, the uses of retroreflective materials are many. They are purchased in very large quantities by government agencies for use on highways. They are applied to bicycles and motor vehicles to make them more visible at night. And they assist pilots by improving the visibility of runway markers.

Some uses for retroreflective materials are not related to safety. For example, these materials play a key role in helping railroads locate and make maximum use of their rolling stock. Color-coded retroreflective numerals, strips or dots applied to the side of railway cars identify the cars by their individual inventory numbers and by the particular type of car. Optical scanners "read" and record this information as the train passes by, thus making it possible for railroad management to locate an individual car or to determine the distribution of boxcars throughout the rail network.

Large sums are spent for retroreflective materials, but purchasers have often found it difficult to specify performance for the materials they buy. Performance is of concern not only from the standpoint of the brightness of reflected light, but also from the standpoint of its color. It is important, for example, that the yellow hues used in warning signals be of consistent color quality on all road signs so the driver can rely on color, as well as shape, to discern the signs' meanings. Seven colors—silver, blue, yellow, red, green, brown and orange—are currently used for marking the interstate highway system.

Since 1971 the National Bureau of Standards has been working to develop instrumental test methods that could be used to evaluate the performance of retroreflective materials and to aid in the preparation of specifications for their purchase.

Selection 2: Recalling Facts

1. Retroreflective materials are used
   - ☐ a. on planes.
   - ☐ b. on runways.
   - ☐ c. in terminals.

2. Retroreflective materials have been used extensively since the invention of
   - ☐ a. the automobile.
   - ☐ b. the laser beam.
   - ☐ c. photography.

3. Optical scanners are used by
   - ☐ a. some railroads.
   - ☐ b. many opticians.
   - ☐ c. computer scientists.

4. Which retroreflective color is not used on interstate highways?
   - ☐ a. Silver
   - ☐ b. Purple
   - ☐ c. Brown

5. The National Bureau of Standards began work on retroreflective devices in
   - ☐ a. 1955.
   - ☐ b. 1963.
   - ☐ c. 1971.

Selection 2: Understanding Ideas

6. This article is primarily concerned with
   - ☐ a. technology in photoelectric cells.
   - ☐ b. retroreflection and tropism in animals and insects.
   - ☐ c. natural and man-made retroreflection.

7. The word predator is used to mean
   - ☐ a. scavenger.
   - ☐ b. wild animal.
   - ☐ c. evil person.

8. An optical scanner is probably
   - ☐ a. a mechanical device.
   - ☐ b. a simple camera.
   - ☐ c. a type of computer.

9. The article suggests that
   - ☐ a. government scientists are developing inexpensive retroreflectors.
   - ☐ b. the government manufactures retroreflective devices.
   - ☐ c. the government buys retroreflective devices from private companies.

10. The reader can conclude that
   - ☐ a. the use of retroreflective material is becoming greater each year.
   - ☐ b. retroreflective paint can be purchased at most hardware stores.
   - ☐ c. retroreflective materials give off light in the dark.

3. Campgrounds

Growth of the commercial campground industry in America closely parallels that of the recreational vehicle industry. As the campground industry rapidly matured, it went through at least three distinct stages of camping developments.

The first stage of private campgrounds, which actually started before World War II, was characterized by small developments of fewer than fifty campsites, built with an average investment of less than $20,000. As more and more people went camping and recreational vehicles became increasingly common, new, well-equipped campgrounds began springing up.

The second stage of commercial campgrounds began about 1964. This was the time when big business entered the camping field. The continued expansion of the recreational vehicle industry had begun to attract the attention of large investors, landowning corporations, motel chains, and oil companies.

While most early campgrounds had been developed as a source of extra income on land already owned by the developer, new investors were now looking for land to buy in the right locations for attracting campers. At the same time, franchising entered the scene and provided chains of campgrounds all across the country.

Campgrounds of the second stage were bigger and contained nearly 100 campsites. They were more expensive to develop, and they offered a larger array of services and facilities, such as stores, recreation halls, laundromats, and supervised recreation programs. Full utility connections for recreation vehicles became common.

The late 1960s and early 1970s saw the introduction of commercial camping's third stage, the "resort campground." Because of large development expense, most resort campgrounds were found in Florida and similar areas where a year-long camping season is assured. However, there are a few in such northern states as Maine and Michigan. These "campgrounds" provide the ultimate in services: marinas, gas stations, restaurants, movies, water sports, golf and tennis, sports instruction, craft and souvenir shops, baby tending, and even discotheque bars. Built on exceptionally attractive water bodies, these campsites have fees that vary from as much as $16 for a waterfront site to a low $5 or $6 well back from the water.

One of the most recent innovations in the third stage of campgrounds is the condominium campground where a camper can buy a campsite and pay an annual maintenance fee for campground upkeep. The condominium offers some of the comfort and convenience of a second home, without the high initial investment and taxes that characterize most resort communities.

Selection 3: Recalling Facts

1. About how many stages of development has camping undergone?
   - ☐ a. Three
   - ☐ b. Four
   - ☐ c. Five

2. The first stage of private campground building began just before
   - ☐ a. World War I.
   - ☐ b. World War II.
   - ☐ c. the Korean War.

3. The resort campground was developed during the late
   - ☐ a. 1940s.
   - ☐ b. 1950s.
   - ☐ c. 1960s.

4. Most resort campgrounds are found in the state of
   - ☐ a. California.
   - ☐ b. Florida.
   - ☐ c. New Mexico.

5. Resort campgrounds can cost as little as
   - ☐ a. $5 per day.
   - ☐ b. $8 per day.
   - ☐ c. $12 per day.

Selection 3: Understanding Ideas

6. According to the article, the state of Maine
   - ☐ a. has the greatest number of oceanfront campgrounds.
   - ☐ b. was the first state to build campgrounds.
   - ☐ c. has a few resort campgrounds.

7. The advantage of a condominium campground is that
   - ☐ a. it offers more privacy than other campgrounds.
   - ☐ b. there are no property taxes.
   - ☐ c. many people share the mortgage expenses.

8. As campgrounds became numerous,
   - ☐ a. they competed for business by lowering their fees.
   - ☐ b. they offered more services and facilities.
   - ☐ c. they remained open during the winter months.

9. Each year condominium campers are expected
   - ☐ a. to participate in community activities.
   - ☐ b. to pay for maintenance services.
   - ☐ c. to serve on the governing board.

10. The author implies that
    - ☐ a. oil companies own stock in the recreation vehicle industry.
    - ☐ b. mobile homes are the most expensive recreation vehicles.
    - ☐ c. tents are no longer as popular as they once were.

4. When Knights Were Bold

From early childhood we are conditioned by rhyme, story, and song to the importance of strong, sturdy construction. This requirement has been drummed into our consciousness from the tragedy of the two little pigs who built their homes of sticks and straw to the storming of an impregnable castle when knights were bold and fortresses were meant to withstand everything short of the atomic bomb.

As we mature and take on the responsibilities of job and family, we are often beset with the task of building our own homes, or castles. This is an awesome task. It is frequently the largest single investment we will ever make.

Again in our minds, the lesson of the three little pigs crops up, and we are bent on finding the builder who will build our house to withstand the ravages of use and time. Thus begins the search for the man or team of men who can transform our house plans and dreams into full-scale, three-dimensional ideal space for living.

If an individual has already purchased and paid for his lot and has acquired the plans and specifications of his dream home, the next step is the engaging of a building contractor to produce it.

Perhaps an individual has had a previous successful experience with a building contracting firm in the community or has friends or acquaintances who have recently completed their homes and have been pleased with the contractor's results. If this is the case, the search for a builder may be of short duration.

But that is not the usual case. Ordinarily, in small residential work, a selected list of bidders is made up consisting of qualified and experienced contractors. They are invited to submit a lump sum bid for which they will complete the work.

The list of bidders should consist of about five firms. Selection of contractors to make up this list may be difficult if a family is new in the community or has had no contact with the building industry.

In the event one has engaged complete architectural services for his home, his architect is in a position to recommend builders who have undertaken similar projects from his office and who are reliable, reputable and good builders. If this is not the case, however, one will have to rely on recommendations from friends and others who have recently had something built.

Selection 4: Recalling Facts

1. The author mentions the story of
   - ☐ a. the little pigs. ☐ b. Cinderella. ☐ c. Sir Lancelot.

2. A person who actually builds a house is called
   - ☐ a. an architect. ☐ b. an engineer. ☐ c. a contractor.

3. Most building contracts are assigned as a result of
   - ☐ a. personal recommendations.
   - ☐ b. competitive bids.
   - ☐ c. previous work.

4. According to the author, building a home is
   - ☐ a. an exciting adventure.
   - ☐ b. an awesome task.
   - ☐ c. a complex operation.

5. How many bids are usually taken for a construction job?
   - ☐ a. Three ☐ b. Five ☐ c. Seven

Selection 4: Understanding Ideas

6. Children's rhymes, stories, and songs stress the importance of
   - ☐ a. large homes. ☐ b. tasteful decor. ☐ c. sturdy construction.

7. In the article the author mentions a house made of
   - ☐ a. bricks. ☐ b. sticks. ☐ c. stones.

8. The search for a builder is most time-consuming when
   - ☐ a. a person is new to a community.
   - ☐ b. a large house is to be built.
   - ☐ c. a person plans to build a home in a remote area.

9. A bid usually consists of
   - ☐ a. itemized lists of construction costs.
   - ☐ b. one price for the entire job.
   - ☐ c. a cost estimate of materials only.

10. When the author mentions children's nursery stories,
    - ☐ a. he is showing the origins of certain attitudes.
    - ☐ b. he is discussing the history of entertainment.
    - ☐ c. he is implying that children are imaginative.

5. Schizophrenia: Is There a Cure?

Schizophrenia is no longer viewed as a chronic, progressive, hopeless disease. Many schizophrenic patients improve to such an extent that they lead independent, satisfying lives. Indeed, they may even grow from the experience to become fuller human beings. To do so, they integrate the experience into their lives instead of trying to ignore it. The schizophrenic experience is so powerful that it is almost certain to have a crucial impact on an individual's life. Trying to forget it is not only difficult, but detrimental; trying to accept it and learn from it is also exceedingly difficult, but potentially growth enhancing. In this sense, a schizophrenic episode can be a creative experience.

However, there is no single cure for schizophrenia. No simple operation, no single drug, no instant magic has been found. Unrealistic expectations followed by equally great disappointments have frequently led to despair and the consequent neglect of schizophrenics.

Indeed, it is probably unrealistic to expect cure in the sense of complete restoration to former functioning. That is rarely expected of any branch of medicine. X-rays reveal that even a completely healed broken leg, for example, shows bone changes associated with healing. Thus, in the absolute sense, the broken leg is not cured but repaired. Applying this analogy to the recovered sehizophrenic, one would expect scars or changes from previous characteristics. When a man comes out of the hospital or other treatment center, one should not expect that he will be the same as he was before the disorder. Much as a survivor of a fire, he has lived through a powerful experience, and one should not expect him to remain untouched by it.

Perhaps the greatest roadblock to recovery a schizophrenic faces is a lack of attention from others. They may fear, for example, that a small patch of irrationality within him may someday expand until, unchecked, it dominates his personality. Given the almost universal fear of losing one's mind, it is small wonder that society too often neglects the schizophrenic and keeps him at a distance. Unfortunately, this distance only reinforces the schizophrenic's difficulty with relationships and will, therefore, tend to reinforce his illness.

It is generally best to seek advice first from a family doctor, or from a local medical society that can recommend a physician, clinic, or psychiatrist. Schizophrenia is treatable and in most instances the treatment can allow return to a normal life within a fairly short period of time.

Selection 5: Recalling Facts

1. The author says that a schizophrenic episode can be
   □ a. permanent.   □ b. disorienting.   □ c. creative.

2. People usually treat a schizophrenic with
   □ a. hostility.   □ b. wonderment.   □ c. caution.

3. A doctor would probably advise a person with schizophrenia
   □ a. to forget it.   □ b. to ignore it.   □ c. to accept it.

4. A person with symptoms of schizophrenia should
   □ a. tell friends.   □ b. seek help.   □ c. take medication.

5. Schizophrenics who look for magical cures are usually
   □ a. grateful.   □ b. disappointed.   □ c. satisfied.

Selection 5: Understanding Ideas

6. Schizophrenia today is considered
   □ a. a chronic disease.
   □ b. a constructive experience.
   □ c. a progressive illness.

7. The author says that schizophrenia
   □ a. can be cured completely.
   □ b. is best treated with X-rays.
   □ c. leaves permanent scars.

8. The author warns the reader about people who
   □ a. are sympathetic towards schizophrenics.
   □ b. have a history of schizophrenia.
   □ c. say they have a cure for schizophrenia.

9. The author compares a schizophrenic to
   □ a. a survivor of a fire.
   □ b. a person with amnesia.
   □ c. a child learning to walk.

10. The author is
    □ a. sarcastic toward schizophrenics.
    □ b. disappointed with hospital care.
    □ c. critical of society.

6. Scientists or Dreamers?

Reading Time _____

Comprehension Score _____

Words per Minute _____

People the world over speak of the Space Age as beginning with the launching of the Russian Sputnik on October 4, 1957. Yet Americans might set the date back to July 1955, when the White House, through President Eisenhower's press secretary, announced that the United States planned to launch a man-made earth satellite. If the undertaking seemed bizarre to the American public at that time, to astrophysicists and some of the military the government's decision was a source of elation. After years of waiting, they had won official support for a project that promised to provide an invaluable tool for basic research in the regions beyond the upper atmosphere. Six weeks later, after a statement came from the Pentagon that the Navy was to take charge of the launching program, most Americans apparently forgot about it. It did not assume great importance again until October 1957.

Every major scientific advance has depended upon two basic elements. The first is the imaginative perception; the second is continually refined tools to observe, measure, and record phenomena that support, alter, or demolish a tentative hypothesis. This process of basic research often seems to have no immediate utility, but it is essential to progress in any field. In space exploration, the data fed back to scientists from instrumented satellites have been of utmost importance. The continuing improvement of such research opens up the prospect of greatly enlarging knowledge of the world we live in and making new applications of that knowledge.

In the decade before Sputnik, however, laymen tended to ridicule the idea of putting a man-made object into orbit around the earth. Even if the feat were possible, what purpose would it serve except to show that it could be done? As early as 1903, Konstantin Tsiolkovsky, a Russian scientist, had proved mathematically the feasibility of using the reactive force that lifts a rocket to eject a vehicle into space above the pull of the earth's gravity. Twenty years later, Romanian-born Hermann Oberth had independently worked out similar formulas. Before the 1950s, the studies of both men remained virtually unknown in the English-speaking world. Neither had built a usable rocket to demonstrate the validity of his theories; and, preoccupied as each was with plans for human journeys to the moon and planets, neither had so much as mentioned an unmanned, artificial satellite.

Selection 6: Recalling Facts

1. Sputnik was launched in
   ☐ a. 1952. ☐ b. 1957. ☐ c. 1962.

2. To the American public, the first American launch seemed
   ☐ a. wasteful. ☐ b. overdue. ☐ c. bizarre.

3. Responsibility for the American launch program was assumed by
   ☐ a. the Army. ☐ b. the Navy. ☐ c. the Air Force.

4. Tsiolkovsky and Oberth never discussed
   ☐ a. moon trips. ☐ b. artificial satellites. ☐ c. reactive forces.

5. Hermann Oberth was born in
   ☐ a. Romania. ☐ b. Poland. ☐ c. Hungary.

Selection 6: Understanding Ideas

6. The author points out that Tsiolkovsky and Oberth
   ☐ a. never accepted the concept of escaping the earth's gravity.
   ☐ b. never built a usable rocket to prove their theories.
   ☐ c. never had help in their laboratory work.

7. Tsiolkovsky proved that
   ☐ a. a rocket could be lifted into space.
   ☐ b. solid fuel could be manufactured from known substances.
   ☐ c. the distance to the moon was equal to the earth's axis ratio.

8. The work of Tsiolkovsky and Oberth was
   ☐ a. published in England against their wishes.
   ☐ b. kept secret for many years.
   ☐ c. made known after their deaths.

9. The first person to prove the feasibility of rocketry was
   ☐ a. Goddard. ☐ b. Oberth. ☐ c. Tsiolkovsky.

10. We can conclude that the American Space Age
    ☐ a. began in the Kennedy Administration.
    ☐ b. could have begun earlier than the Russian.
    ☐ c. was based on the success of the Russian program.

7. A Potent Weapon

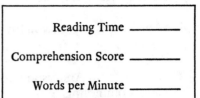

Reading Time _____

Comprehension Score _____

Words per Minute _____

Besides the unhealthful, debilitating prison conditions, the Federal soldiers in Andersonville had to contend with depredations by their own comrades who frequently stole food, clothing, and whatever other valuables they could lay their hands on and who used violence to gain their ends. The Andersonville Raiders, a large, organized group of thieves and murderers, were the most notorious and dangerous predators. For nearly four months the Raiders held sway inside the prison, and robberies and murders were daily occurrences. Finally, with the help of prison officials, the six ringleaders were captured. On July 11, 1864, after a quick trial by fellow inmates, they were hanged.

Because the prison was situated far from Union lines and because the dogs, used by the Confederates to track runaways, were efficient, escape from Andersonville was difficult. During the prison's existence, 329 prisoners escaped. Most of these slipped away while on work details outside the stockade.

When the emaciated survivors of Andersonville returned to their homes at the end of the war, there was widespread demand in the North for the punishment of those responsible for what many claimed were deliberately planned atrocities. Next to the assassination of President Abraham Lincoln, the Andersonville story was the most potent weapon in the arsenal of those who wished to impose a harsh reconstruction on the former Confederate States of America.

Despite numerous claims to the contrary, there was no conspiracy on the part of Confederate officials to deliberately exterminate the Federal soldiers confined at Andersonville. The horrors of Andersonville resulted principally from the breakdown of the Southern economy. Throughout the Civil War the Confederacy suffered from three fundamental weaknesses that crippled her military operations and made the functioning of an efficient prisoner-of-war system virtually impossible. Because industrial output was inadequate for support of the armed forces, military prisons were extremely primitive in their construction, equipment, and maintenance. Second, the Quartermaster and Commissary Corps, for various reasons, were never able to properly clothe and feed the Confederate Army, let alone prisoners of war. Finally, after the first two years of war, rail and water transportation were so crippled that the movement of supplies to peripheral points in the Confederacy was frequently cut off. Andersonville was one of those peripheral points.

It is important to recall that almost as many Confederates died in Northern prison camps as the 30,218 Federals who expired in the Southern camps.

Selection 7: Recalling Facts

1. Approximately how many prisoners escaped from Andersonville?
   □ a. 50 □ b. 125 □ c. 300

2. Escape from Andersonville was
   □ a. commonplace. □ b. easy. □ c. difficult.

3. How long did the Andersonville Raiders remain active?
   □ a. Four months □ b. One year □ c. Three years

4. The Andersonville Raiders were
   □ a. Southern militia men.
   □ b. Northern prisoners.
   □ c. Confederate prison guards.

5. The horrors of Andersonville resulted primarily from the breakdown of the
   □ a. U.S. judicial system. □ b. Southern economy. □ c. Northern resistance.

Selection 7: Understanding Ideas

6. The Andersonville Raiders were most notorious for their
   □ a. capturing of escaped prisoners.
   □ b. surprise raids on enemy camps.
   □ c. killing and stealing within the prison.

7. The author suggests that
   □ a. many prisoners made unsuccessful escape attempts from the prison.
   □ b. Northern troops were better trained than Confederate troops.
   □ c. the Confederate Army was well clothed and well fed.

8. From the information provided, we can assume that
   □ a. Confederate officials conspired to exterminate Federal soldiers.
   □ b. Andersonville suffered from severe shortages of supplies.
   □ c. Andersonville was the center of Southern military operations.

9. The assassination of Abraham Lincoln is mentioned as an example of
   □ a. distorted newspaper reporting.
   □ b. an alleged Southern atrocity.
   □ c. history repeating itself.

10. We can conclude that
    □ a. conditions in Andersonville were no worse than those in Northern prisons.
    □ b. the construction of Andersonville weakened the Confederate Army.
    □ c. slavery was the primary cause of the Civil War.

8. Federal Jobs Overseas

United States citizens are employed by the federal government in Alaska, Hawaii, United States territories, and in foreign countries. They are found in almost every occupational field. They are construction and maintenance workers, doctors, nurses, teachers, technical experts, mining engineers, meteorologists, clerks, stenographers, typists, geologists, skilled tradesmen, social workers, agricultural marketing specialists, and agricultural and other economists.

Current needs of agencies with jobs to fill are generally limited to highly qualified and hard-to-find professional personnel, skilled technicians, and, in some cases, stenographers and clerical and administrative personnel. A few agencies are seeking experienced teachers, librarians, nurses, and medical personnel. However, a few vacancies occur in most fields because of normal turnover in personnel.

Most vacancies are filled by the appointment of local eligibles who qualify in competitive civil-service examinations which are announced and held in the local area. Normally, there is a sufficient local labor market to fill the needs and examinations are not publicized outside the local areas. Some positions, however, may be filled by transferring career government employees from the United States mainland.

When a vacancy is to be filled in a foreign country, a decision is made whether to recruit from among persons in the area where the job is located or to seek qualified applicants residing in the United States. If the position is to be filled locally, the appointee may be a United States citizen residing or traveling in the area, the wife or dependent of a citizen employed or stationed in the area, or a foreign national.

In most instances where United States installations are established in foreign countries, either formal or informal agreements have been drawn up assuring the host government that local nationals will be employed wherever possible in order to be of maximum assistance to the economy of that country. Furthermore, it is almost always to the economic advantage of the United States to employ foreign nationals at local pay rates without responsibility for travel costs and overseas cost-of-living allowances. Positions held by foreign nationals are in the excepted service and are not subject to the competitive requirements of the Civil Service Act and rules.

However, there are many thousands of technical, administrative, and supervisory positions in which United States citizens are employed in foreign countries. These positions are usually in the competitive service, and, as vacancies occur, they are filled in most cases by transferring career government employees from the United States.

Selection 8: Recalling Facts

1. The primary advantage to hiring foreign nationals involves
   □ a. salary.   □ b. working conditions. □ c. advancements.

2. Civil-service examinations are held in
   □ a. Washington, D.C.   □ b. capital cities.   □ c. local areas.

3. Vacancies most often occur because of
   □ a. normal turnover.   □ b. serious illnesses.   □ c. frequent resignations.

4. A foreign national working for the U.S. is not subject to
   □ a. civil-service rules.
   □ b. his own government.
   □ c. U.S. laws.

5. The author calls civil-service examinations
   □ a. competitive.   □ b. difficult.   □ c. unfair.

Selection 8: Understanding Ideas

6. This article is about
   □ a. working for the U.S. government.
   □ b. taking civil-service examinations.
   □ c. training to work for the government abroad.

7. If a person wants a government job outside the U.S., he must
   □ a. take an exam.
   □ b. sign a work contract.
   □ c. apply in person.

8. At the present time, the government has particular need for
   □ a. high school graduates.
   □ b. men and women under 40.
   □ c. highly qualified specialists.

9. This article implies that the better-paying government jobs
   □ a. do not usually have vacancies.
   □ b. are sometimes available for qualified people.
   □ c. usually have a surplus of applicants.

10. In an agricultural nation, a local national would work
    □ a. on a U.S. military base.
    □ b. on a sugar plantation.
    □ c. in an industrial plant.

9. The Food Web

Reading Time _____

Comprehension Score _____

Words per Minute _____

A brief look at the abundance of marine plant and animal life and how each kind relates to the others shows that the sea is much more productive than one visualizes.

Many parts of the ocean contain vast pastures of tiny, drifting plant life called phytoplankton. As in plant life on land, chlorophyll in the phytoplankton has the ability to convert the sun's energy into organic substances using simple dissolved nutrients in the surrounding water. In some places in the ocean, phytoplankton is so abundant that it changes the natural blue color of the water to shades of green, brown, or even red. Microscopic phytoplankton is the basic food that supports all ● aquatic life.

The next level in the food web consists of grazing animals, many also very tiny. These small creatures, known as zooplankton, range in size from simple one-celled microscopic animals to more complex and abundant forms, like fish larvae, copepods, and somewhat larger shrimplike euphausids. Free-swimming copepods, perhaps more than any other animal, eat tiny phytoplankton and convert an otherwise inaccessible food supply into a form readily available to larger animals. To indicate how abundant zooplankton is, baleen whales, the largest animals in the world, also feed on small animals, and their stomachs may often contain tons of euphausids. ●

Feeding on zooplankton and also on microscopic plants are the filter-feeding fishes. The gill arches of these fishes have comblike filaments that strain plankton from the water. Good examples of the filter-feeders are the sardine and anchovy, which are among the smaller fishes of the sea and also the most plentiful.

Feeding on the smaller abundant fishes are larger fishes. A mackerel illustrates this level in the food web.

Finally, the top layer in the food web consists of large, carnivorous predators, like tunas, swordfish, and sharks.

The food web is an oversimplification of much more complicated processes and ● interactions. It serves, however, to illustrate that, at each higher level of the web, a smaller and smaller quantity of fish or shellfish is present in the ocean.

Fishery experts believe that the marine harvest can be increased at least five times to give the world a catch of 550 billion pounds. This may be achieved if we change our fishing and processing methods and our fish-eating habits to use effectively the vast numbers of marine animals not now being caught.

Selection 9: Recalling Facts

1. According to the author, phytoplankton can be found
   □ a. clinging to rocks.
   □ b. drifting in the water.
   □ c. growing at great depths.

2. The second step in the food web consists of
   □ a. phytoplankton.   □ b. filter-feeders.   □ c. zooplankton.

3. Baleen whales usually feed on
   □ a. euphausids.   □ b. copepods.   □ c. shrimp.

4. The most plentiful fish in the oceans is
   □ a. the tuna.   □ b. the shark.   □ c. the sardine.

5. Fishery experts believe that the marine harvest can be increased
   □ a. 300 percent.   □ b. 400 percent.   □ c. 500 percent.

Selection 9: Understanding Ideas

6. Phytoplankton is important because
   □ a. it consumes pollutants in the oceans.
   □ b. it adds carbon dioxide to the water.
   □ c. it is the basic food for many fish.

7. Baleen whales are cited as examples of
   □ a. the most dangerous animals in the sea.
   □ b. the largest animals in the world.
   □ c. the most endangered species in the sea.

8. The author develops his discussion according to
   □ a. order of size.
   □ b. order of importance.
   □ c. order of time.

9. At the highest level of the food web,
   □ a. the population density is much less than at lower levels.
   □ b. the animals are more beneficial to man.
   □ c. the problem of extinction becomes more serious.

10. The author implies that
   □ a. the governments of the world should control sport fishing.
   □ b. whale-killing should not be sanctioned by any country of the world.
   □ c. mankind should learn to eat lower forms of sea life.

10. Keeping It Clean

Reading Time _____

Comprehension Score _____

Words per Minute _____

From the time of George Washington our Presidents have been interested in the Potomac. But not before February 1965 did a President take a positive stand on the total watershed and its future.

In a "Message on the Natural Beauty of our Country," President Lyndon B. Johnson stated that the Potomac should become a model of both conservation and beauty for the nation. The President directed the Secretary of the Interior to develop a plan to "clean up the river and keep it clean," to protect the natural beauty of the river and its basin, and to assure a supply of water from the river and other sources to meet municipal needs for the decades ahead. The plan also had to provide adequate flood control and to give maximum recreational opportunities to people who live along the river or its tributaries and to those who visit the river basin.

Judging from the *Potomac Interim Report to the President,* published a year later in January 1966, the Interdepartmental Task Force, which was established to develop the plan, decided to first draw up a master plan for recreation. The plan provided for recreation and natural beauty by requiring high levels of water quality and public control of access to the river and its major tributaries, through easement or ownership of the flood plains and the shoreline.

For the Potomac to become the model conservation and recreation success which the President expected, the quality of the water in the river had to improve significantly. There had to be more rigid limitations on the amounts of organic pollutants entering this river and sediment had to be kept out of the Potomac by effective erosion control measures.

The model plan for the Potomac is abundantly clear. The plan is an expression of demand—primarily a demand for the water-based recreation which already has been mentioned.

And this recreation requirement stems principally from the pressing needs of the Washington, D.C., region where two-thirds of the basin's 3.5 million population lives without many satisfactory opportunities for outdoor recreation. While offending accuracy somewhat—for the sake of simplicity—one can fairly say that the model plan represents but another chapter in a lengthy catalog of demands which, in this century, Washington, D.C., and its suburbs have placed on the water and the land resources of the far-flung Potomac Basin.

Selection 10: Recalling Facts

1. The first President to take a positive stand on the Potomac River issue was
   □ a. Truman. □ b. Kennedy. □ c. Johnson.

2. The project of cleaning the Potomac River was assigned to
   □ a. the Department of the Interior.
   □ b. the Department of Agriculture.
   □ c. the Department of State.

3. The first master plan for the Potomac was concerned with
   □ a. irrigation. □ b. municipal water. □ c. recreation.

4. Over the years sediment accumulated in the river because of
   □ a. erosion. □ b. chemical dumping. □ c. residential misuse.

5. About how many people live in the Potomac River basin?
   □ a. 2 million □ b. 3.5 million □ c. 5 million

Selection 10: Understanding Ideas

6. The article implies that the Potomac River
   □ a. was more polluted than the Mississippi River.
   □ b. flows by Washington, D. C.
   □ c. supplies drinking water to several communities.

7. Recreational facilities along the Potomac
   □ a. will include several large tennis courts.
   □ b. will not allow hunting or swimming.
   □ c. will be open to out-of-state tourists.

8. The author implies that the Potomac River
   □ a. has threatened lowland areas with flooding.
   □ b. will furnish hydroelectric power to a large area.
   □ c. was cut into the landscape by the retreating ice sheet.

9. The *Potomac Interim Report to the President*
   □ a. was drawn up under the supervision of the Vice-President.
   □ b. required twelve months of research to complete.
   □ c. amounted to three large volumes of material.

10. We can conclude that
    □ a. water pollution is reversible.
    □ b. polluted water can be used for agricultural purposes.
    □ c. the Potomac River basin has become a wildlife refuge.

11. Curds and Whey

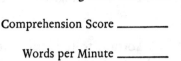

Reading Time _____

Comprehension Score _____

Words per Minute _____

Many countries have developed one or more varieties of cheese peculiar to their own conditions and culture.

When the colonists settled in the New World, they brought with them their own methods of making their favorite kinds of cheese. The first Cheddar cheese factory in the United States was built by Jesse Williams, near Rome, Oneida County, N.Y., in 1851. As the population increased in the East and there was a corresponding increase in the demand for market milk, the cheese industry gradually moved westward. Cheesemaking in the United States and in the other leading cheese-producing countries of the world is now largely a factory industry.

Many of the popular varieties, although originating in Europe, are now produced in the United States and are available in most food stores, delicatessens and specialty cheese stores.

The making of natural cheese is an art centuries old. It consists of separating most of the milk solids from the milk by curdling with rennet or bacterial culture or both and separating the curd from the whey by heating, stirring, and pressing. Most cheeses in this country are made from whole milk. For certain types of cheese both milk and cream are used. For other types, skim milk, whey or mixtures of all of these are used.

The distinctive flavor, body, and texture characteristics of the various cheeses are the results of the kind of milk used; the method used for curdling the milk and for cutting, cooking, and forming the curd; the type of bacteria or molds used in ripening; the amount of salt or other seasonings added and the conditions of ripening such as temperature, humidity and length of time. Sometimes only minor differences in the procedures followed may make the difference between one variety of cheese and another.

After the cheese has been formed into its characteristic shape, it is given a coating of wax or other protective coating or wrapping. It is then allowed to cure or age for varying lengths of time depending upon the kind or variety of cheese being made.

When the cheese has reached its proper curing stage, it is often cut or sliced from larger blocks or wheels into more suitable sizes for consumer use. The refrigerated showcase in a modern food market is most enticing with its display of various shapes and sizes of cheese packages such as wedges, oblongs, cubes, slices, and blocks.

Selection 11: Recalling Facts

1. The first Cheddar cheese factory in the U.S. was built in
   ☐ a. Maryland.   ☐ b. New York.   ☐ c. Virginia.

2. According to the article, rennet is used
   ☐ a. to curdle milk.   ☐ b. to sour milk.   ☐ c. to produce bacteria.

3. Most cheeses in this country are made from
   ☐ a. cream.   ☐ b. skim milk.   ☐ c. whole milk.

4. What ingredient is added to most cheeses?
   ☐ a. Salt   ☐ b. Yeast   ☐ c. Monosodium glutamate

5. The first Cheddar cheese factory in the U.S. was built during the middle
   ☐ a. 1600s.   ☐ b. 1700s.   ☐ c. 1800s.

Selection 11: Understanding Ideas

6. This article is mostly about
   ☐ a. manufacturing cheese.
   ☐ b. buying and storing cheese.
   ☐ c. importing cheeses from Europe.

7. The article implies that
   ☐ a. most people do not like strong cheeses.
   ☐ b. the U.S. is one of the largest cheese-producing countries.
   ☐ c. Wisconsin produces more cheese than any other state.

8. The cheese industry moved westward
   ☐ a. as the need for cheaper labor became apparent.
   ☐ b. as the raising of cattle became more common in the West.
   ☐ c. as the demand for milk increased in the East.

9. The reader can infer that whey is
   ☐ a. thin and watery.
   ☐ b. smooth and creamy.
   ☐ c. thick and lumpy.

10. We can conclude from this article that
    ☐ a. many factors influence the flavor of cheese.
    ☐ b. cheese is very high in protein.
    ☐ c. Cheddar cheese originated in America.

12. Land of Ice and Snow

For many years, Antarctica was thought to be only an archipelago whose islands were tied together above sea level by ice. It was thought to be made up of two small subcontinents—East Antarctica, the larger, and West Antarctica, containing the Antarctic Peninsula. The two continents were supposed to be separated by a large trough, below sea level, that connected the Ross and Weddell Seas.

Geophysical studies have now revealed a fairly complete picture of the Antarctic landform below its ice cover. We know now that West Antarctica is connected to the main part of the continent by a chain of mountains well above sea level, though largely buried by ice and snow. The bedrock of much of East Antarctica appears to be above sea level. Some of it, in high ranges of the Transantarctic Mountains, is far above sea level.

Whether mineral wealth lies hidden by the vast ice sheets is unknown. No more than 2 percent of the continent is actual rock outcrop and much of this small and probably unrepresentative sample has yet to be visited by geologists. Certainly no deposits rich enough to be economically useful have been found.

Geologists now know that the ice-buried rocks of the Antarctic are similar to rocks of the other continents of the world. Minor amounts of potentially valuable minerals have been reported. The presence of petroleum has been speculated upon by several geologists, but none has yet been found. Low-grade deposits of coal are widespread, especially in the Transantarctic Mountains, but there has been no attempt at exploitation. Even if rich mineral deposits were to be found in Antarctica, the cost of removal from this remote and inhospitable land would be exorbitant.

Interpretation of continental structure is an important objective of any extensive geologic investigation. Yet except for the earth's ocean basins, no area the size of Antarctica is so geologically unknown. With 98 percent of the continent covered by ice, it is extremely difficult to decipher the continent's general structure. Geologists determine geologic structure by studying rock outcrops, and many of these are small and widely separated. No outcrops are known in the vast interior of East Antarctica.

Working out the continental structure of Antarctica is analogous to learning that of the entire United States from studies of a few scattered counties in California and mountain ranges scattered at irregular intervals across the country.

Selection 12: Recalling Facts

1. Little is known about Antarctica's
   - ☐ a. climate.
   - ☐ b. landform and size.
   - ☐ c. mineral wealth.

2. How much of Antarctica is covered by ice?
   - ☐ a. 52 percent
   - ☐ b. 76 percent
   - ☐ c. 98 percent

3. Antarctica is made up of
   - ☐ a. several islands.
   - ☐ b. two subcontinents.
   - ☐ c. connected land masses.

4. In Antarctica, petroleum
   - ☐ a. is common.
   - ☐ b. cannot form.
   - ☐ c. may be present.

5. Low-grade deposits of coal have been found in Antarctica's
   - ☐ a. valleys.
   - ☐ b. coastline.
   - ☐ c. mountains.

Selection 12: Understanding Ideas

6. This article is concerned primarily with
   - ☐ a. the exploration for minerals in Antarctica.
   - ☐ b. the geological composition of Antarctica.
   - ☐ c. the establishment of the first geophysical laboratory.

7. The author implies that Antarctica
   - ☐ a. is a group of separate islands.
   - ☐ b. consists of two separate islands.
   - ☐ c. is really one large island.

8. The author suggests that geologists
   - ☐ a. study rocks with little difficulty in Antarctica.
   - ☐ b. find ice and snow to be a problem in rock study.
   - ☐ c. have never tried to extract minerals from Antarctica.

9. California is mentioned by the author
   - ☐ a. to illustrate the type of rock found in Antarctica.
   - ☐ b. to show the difficulty in mapping the structure of Antarctica.
   - ☐ c. to provide an example of uniform climate.

10. We may conclude that
   - ☐ a. Antarctica will someday supply the world's mineral needs.
   - ☐ b. geophysical studies of Antarctica are now complete.
   - ☐ c. controversy exists on the geological composition of Antarctica.

13. Buy, Use and Discard

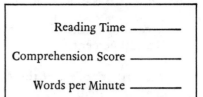

Reading Time _____

Comprehension Score _____

Words per Minute _____

The free enterprise system has produced a technology capable of providing the American consumer with the largest and most varied marketplace in the world. Technological advances, however, have come hand-in-hand with impersonal mass marketing of goods and services. Along with progress, too, have come some instances of manipulative advertising practices and a proliferation of products whose reliability, safety and quality are difficult to evaluate.

Today's consumers buy, enjoy, use and discard more types of goods than could possibly have been imagined even a few years ago. Yet too often consumers have no idea of the materials that have gone into the manufacturer's finished product or their own motivation in selecting one product over another.

Easy credit and forceful techniques of modern marketing persuade many consumers to buy what they cannot afford. The consequent overburdening of family budgets is a problem for consumers at all economic levels. It is not unusual for families to allocate 20 percent or more of their income to debt repayments without understanding the effect this allocation has upon other choices. Some families have such tight budgets that an illness, a period of unemployment, or some other crisis finds them without adequate reserves.

In addition to the growing complexity of the market, consumers are sometimes faced with unfair and deceptive practices. Although there are laws designed to protect the consumer, there is not a sufficient number of law enforcers to cover all the abuses of the marketplace.

There is growing concern and awareness, too, of the disadvantage of the poor and undereducated American in the marketplace of the affluent. Families in low-income inner city and rural areas often do not have the same varieties of goods and prices available to them as their middle-income counterparts. They are more likely to be targets for fraudulent sales schemes and high cost credit than their affluent neighbors.

An adult in today's society should be knowledgeable in the use of credit. He should understand what is involved in purchasing a house, and the many pitfalls to be avoided when entering into financial agreements. He should know enough about advertising and selling techniques to enable him to discern the honest from the fraudulent and deceptive. He should be knowledgeable about consumer protection laws so that he can demand his rights. When he needs help, he should know the private and public sources to which he can turn for assistance.

Selection 13: Recalling Facts

1. According to the author, many families overspend by
   ☐ a. 20 percent.   ☐ b. 30 percent.   ☐ c. 40 percent.

2. The author feels that the American marketplace is
   ☐ a. overrated.   ☐ b. inefficient.   ☐ c. complex.

3. The person who suffers most in the American marketplace is
   ☐ a. the affluent buyer.   ☐ b. the unwise shopper.   ☐ c. the foreign investor.

4. The weakness inherent in the laws designed to protect the consumer is the
   ☐ a. large number of loopholes.
   ☐ b. insufficient number of law enforcers.
   ☐ c. lack of prohibitive penalties.

5. As technology has advanced, mass marketing has become
   ☐ a. impersonal.   ☐ b. formal.   ☐ c. reliable.

Selection 13: Understanding Ideas

6. This article is concerned mostly with
   ☐ a. the free enterprise system in America.
   ☐ b. the difficulty of living on a fixed income.
   ☐ c. innovative techniques in food processing.

7. The author implies that
   ☐ a. products are more expensive in the U.S. than anywhere else.
   ☐ b. credit cards are often used illegally.
   ☐ c. products very often do not perform as advertised.

8. Consumers often do not know
   ☐ a. the brand names of products they buy regularly.
   ☐ b. the current interest rates on savings accounts.
   ☐ c. why they purchase certain products.

9. The author points out that some families
   ☐ a. are unprepared for financial emergencies.
   ☐ b. forget to claim interest charges on their income tax forms.
   ☐ c. spend more money on food than they would like to.

10. The author warns the reader to be cautious when
    ☐ a. buying items on sale.
    ☐ b. buying items on credit.
    ☐ c. buying items at discount.

14. Continental Summers

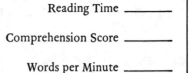

Reading Time _____

Comprehension Score _____

Words per Minute _____

North American summers are hot. As the advancing sun drives back the polar air, the land is opened up to light and solar heat and occupied by masses of moist, warm air spun landward off the tropical ocean. With these rain-filled visitors come the tongues of dry desert air that flick northward out of Mexico and, occasionally, the hot winds that howl down the Rockies' eastern slopes.

Inequalities of atmospheric heating and cooling, of moistness and aridity, are regulated at middle latitudes by horizontal and vertical mixing. The mixing apparatus is the parade of cyclones, low-pressure centers, and anticyclones, high-pressure centers, which lie at the heart of most weather, good and bad.

The cyclones and anticyclones drift in the mid-latitude westerlies, the prevailing eastward-blowing winds that follow a scalloped path around the northern hemisphere. The large-scale undulations of these winds may extend for thousands of miles and are called planetary waves. Their high-speed core is the jet stream, which snakes across the continent some six to eight miles up, keeping mainly to the cool side of highs and lows as they form, spin, and die below it.

The kind of weather predominating in an area over a period of time depends largely on the prevailing position and orientation of the jet stream. As the continent warms, the jet stream shifts northward, along with the tracks of surface weather disturbances. Cyclones bring June thundershowers to the Plains. The humid spring of Georgia becomes the muggy summer of Illinois. These alternations of instability, hot and cool, moist and dry, combine annually to generate the average summer climate for North America.

When these alternating processes are somehow interrupted, the climatic "norm" of summer is marred by a heat wave. The anomaly is usually associated with a change in the planetary waves, so that the prevailing winds from the southwestern deserts sweep farther north than usual and blanket a large region with hot, often humid, air at ground level. An upper-level high may settle over the mid-continent, destroying cloud cover with its descending, compression-heated currents, until the blessing of fair weather turns to the curse of drought. In addition, heat from the hot, dry ground feeds back into the atmosphere, tending to perpetuate the heat wave circulation.

Whatever the cause, the effect is uncomfortable and dangerous. Continental heat waves live in human memory the way fierce winters do.

Selection 14: Recalling Facts

1. North American summers are considered
   ☐ a. mild.   ☐ b. cool.   ☐ c. hot.

2. As summer approaches, the sun drives back
   ☐ a. arctic air masses.   ☐ b. polar air masses.   ☐ c. Pacific air masses.

3. The jet stream is usually found no higher than
   ☐ a. 8 miles.   ☐ b. 125 miles.   ☐ c. 1,600 miles.

4. As summer approaches, the jet stream shifts
   ☐ a. southward.   ☐ b. westward.   ☐ c. northward.

5. An anticyclone is actually
   ☐ a. a low-pressure area. ☐ b. a high-pressure area. ☐ c. a cold front.

Selection 14: Understanding Ideas

6. The author implies that
   ☐ a. there are two systems of weather—upper level and lower level.
   ☐ b. the East coast is susceptible to hurricanes during summer.
   ☐ c. cities are warmer at night than rural areas.

7. The author suggests that changes in climate are the result of
   ☐ a. shifts in the movement of planetary waves.
   ☐ b. advancing low-pressure areas.
   ☐ c. stationary fronts.

8. The author describes the summer season using
   ☐ a. allegory.
   ☐ b. figurative language.
   ☐ c. colloquial language.

9. The author discusses a weather anomaly in the form of
   ☐ a. a heat wave.
   ☐ b. an early snowfall.
   ☐ c. unseasonable rainfall.

10. We can conclude that
    ☐ a. the atmosphere is never stable.
    ☐ b. tornados cannot be predicted accurately.
    ☐ c. summer weather is more predictable than winter weather.

15. Viruses and Cancer

Reading Time _____

Comprehension Score _____

Words per Minute _____

In 1911, a New York scientist succeeded in producing tumors in chickens by inoculating them with a filtrate of tumor tissue containing no cells. His experiments were the first clear demonstration of the role of a virus in one type of malignant tumor. His discovery failed to arouse much interest, however, and only a few workers continued this line of research.

But in the 1930s, two important cancer-virus discoveries were made.

First, scientists succeeded in transmitting a skin wart from a wild rabbit to domestic rabbits by cell-free filtrates. Moreover, in the domestic rabbits the warts were no longer benign, but malignant. As observed with the chickens, the filterable agent, a virus, could seldom be recovered from the malignant tumor which it had induced.

Second, in 1936, workers discovered that breast cancer in offspring of mice occurred only if the mother came from a strain noted for its high incidence of breast cancer. If the father, but not the mother, came from the high cancer line, the young ones did not develop breast cancer. When one of the simplest possibilities was explored—that something was transmitted from the mother to the young after birth—it was found that this something was a virus in the milk of the mothers. When high breast-cancer strain offspring were nursed by low breast-cancer females, the occurrence of cancer was dramatically reduced. In contrast, feeding young mice of low breast-cancer strains with milk from mice of high cancer strains greatly increased the incidence of breast cancer.

Credit for bringing the attention of investigators back to viruses is also probably due to two other discoveries in the 1950s. A scientist showed that mouse leukemia could be transmitted by cell-free filtrates. Newborn animals had to be used for these experiments.

Government scientists have succeeded in isolating from mouse leukemia tissue another agent which has produced salivary gland cancers in mice. After the agent had been grown in tissue culture, it produced many different types of tumors, not only in mice but also in rats and hamsters. This many-tumor virus removed all previous doubts about virus research in cancer. Up until then, it was believed that the few known cancer viruses could each produce only one kind of tumor in one species of animal. Now this concept was shattered, and the question of viruses as a cause of human cancer assumed new significance.

Selection 15: Recalling Facts

1. Filtrates of tumor tissue contain no
   □ a. viruses.   □ b. cells.   □ c. bacteria.

2. The first scientist to produce tumors with filtrates was
   □ a. Russian.   □ b. German.   □ c. American.

3. When one scientist transplanted a wart from one rabbit to another,
   □ a. the donor rabbit died.
   □ b. the benign wart became malignant.
   □ c. the receiver rabbit rejected the tissue.

4. Research with inoculations of filtrates was first conducted on
   □ a. rabbits.   □ b. mice.   □ c. chickens.

5. Doubts about virus cancer ended with the discovery of
   □ a. leukemia filtrates.   □ b. malignant tumors.   □ c. many-tumor viruses.

Selection 15: Understanding Ideas

6. The discoveries mentioned in this article occurred
   □ a. in the late 1800s and early 1900s.
   □ b. in the first quarter of the twentieth century.
   □ c. throughout the 1900s.

7. The author arranges his information according to
   □ a. order of importance.
   □ b. order of interest.
   □ c. chronological order.

8. Government scientists proved that
   □ a. cancer occurs more often in females.
   □ b. cancer can be inherited.
   □ c. cancer viruses can produce different kinds of tumors.

9. The experimentation with breast cancer in mice showed that
   □ a. the tendency to develop cancer can be passed on to children.
   □ b. cancer can be found as a virus in mother's milk.
   □ c. filterable viruses can be recovered from induced tumors.

10. We can conclude that the search for the cause and cure for cancer is
    □ a. a slow and painstaking process.
    □ b. now at a standstill.
    □ c. primarily funded by the government.

16. Youthful Deviancy

Reading Time _____

Comprehension Score _____

Words per Minute _____

No thoughtful community faced by the problems of delinquency can, or should, easily and quickly decide on a course of action. The problem is too complex to be dealt with by any panacea. Yet, the temptation remains strong in many communities to reach for simple but frequently ineffective solutions.

Obviously, no single blueprint can be devised that would apply to all communities. What each community does about curbing youthful deviancy depends in large measure on local needs and capabilities.

One of the first things that each community should do is to determine the amount, scope, and nature of its delinquency problem.

A few bizarre and widely publicized cases *do not* constitute a "crime wave." Local police and court records provide a clear picture of the problem.

These records contain information about the types of offenses reported, as well as when and where they occur. They may also provide information about the age, sex, ethnic-racial, and social class characteristics of known offenders, the disposition of cases and, perhaps, the concentration or dispersion of offenders according to residence or some other geographic reference. Such details about reported offenses and known offenders are essential for developing prevention and control activities.

A differentiation of youthful deviancy according to some sort of classification system is also very helpful. Distinctions between *aberrant, subcultural* and *politically-oriented* behavior are extremely useful for planning purposes.

It is one thing to deal with arson committed by a mentally deranged boy; it is something else to deal with car thefts by gangs of middle-class, "joy-riding" youths; and, it is something else again to deal with the demands of militant young activists.

While many police departments and juvenile courts are capable of providing informed citizens groups with basic statistical information, few are prepared to discuss the problem in more sophisticated terms, or to describe in depth the conditions and malfunctions which may characterize their communities.

One method of providing this information would be for police departments, juvenile courts, and other agencies concerned with the welfare and activities of youth to develop a working relationship with organizations which have demonstrated expertise in this area, such as universities and regional planning groups.

Careful planning also means that special consideration be given to providing services for youth who live in "high-risk" environments.

But whatever ultimate decisions are reached, communities should establish programs that offer a balance between preventive and rehabilitative services.

Selection 16: Recalling Facts

1. The scope and nature of the delinquency problem is seen in
   - ☐ a. bizarre cases.
   - ☐ b. crime waves.
   - ☐ c. court records.

2. According to the author, information about sex, race, age, etc. is
   - ☐ a. unavailable.
   - ☐ b. unnecessary.
   - ☐ c. essential.

3. Most police departments are capable of providing
   - ☐ a. community malfunctions.
   - ☐ b. sophisticated information.
   - ☐ c. basic statistics.

4. One category of youthful deviancy is
   - ☐ a. social behavior.
   - ☐ b. ethnic behavior.
   - ☐ c. subcultural behavior.

5. A crime not mentioned is
   - ☐ a. arson.
   - ☐ b. car thefts.
   - ☐ c. murder.

Selection 16: Understanding Ideas

6. The author seems to feel that
   - ☐ a. one plan for curbing youthful deviancy works well everywhere.
   - ☐ b. universities are out of touch with the juvenile problem.
   - ☐ c. juvenile courts need to become more diversified.

7. The author suggests that communities faced with delinquency should
   - ☐ a. establish a remedial course of action immediately.
   - ☐ b. decide on a course of action slowly and carefully.
   - ☐ c. allow the problem to diminish quietly without publicity.

8. Special considerations should be given to youths living in
   - ☐ a. low socio-economic areas.
   - ☐ b. dangerous environments.
   - ☐ c. potentially risky situations.

9. The author's tone is
   - ☐ a. critical.
   - ☐ b. encouraging.
   - ☐ c. matter-of-fact.

10. We can conclude that
    - ☐ a. local communities have different needs in curbing deviancy.
    - ☐ b. classifying deviancy problems serves no useful purpose.
    - ☐ c. juvenile courts are unable to handle their case loads.

17. Keeping Cool

In the lexicon of violent activities, a cold-blooded deed is one conceived and carried out as dispassionately as a lizard spears a fly. Cold-bloodedness is repugnant to mammals and birds, for they, like humans, are warm-blooded creatures that maintain an essentially constant body temperature regardless of the thermal environment.

To keep on the cool side of their upper thermal limits, human bodies dissipate heat by varying the rate and depth of blood circulation, by losing water through the skin and sweat glands, and, as the last extremity is reached, by panting. Under normal conditions, these reflex activites are kept in balance and controlled by the brain's hypothalamus, a comparatively simple sensor of rising and falling environmental temperatures. It is also a sophisticated manager of temperatures inside.

Like the hot light in a car, the hypothalamus responds to the temperature of the coolant, which in this case is blood. A surge of blood heated above 98.6 degrees sends the hypothalamus into action. As orders of the hypothalamus go out, the heart begins to pump more blood, blood vessels dilate to accommodate the increased flow, and the bundles of tiny capillaries threading through the upper layers of the skin are put into operation. The body's blood is circulated closer to the skin's surface, and excess heat drains off into the cooler atmosphere. At the same time, water diffuses through the skin as insensible perspiration, so called because it evaporates before it becomes visible, and the skin seems dry to the touch.

Heat loss from increased circulation and insensible perspiration is a comparatively minor correction. If the hypothalamus continues to sense overheating, it calls upon the millions of sweat glands which perforate the outer layer of the skin. These tiny glands can shed great quantities of water and heat through perspiration. The skin handles about 90 percent of the body's heat-dissipating function.

As environmental temperature approaches normal body temperature, physical discomfort is replaced by physical danger. The body loses its ability to get rid of heat through the circulatory system, because there is no heat-drawing drop in temperature between the skin and the surrounding air. At this point, the skin's elimination of heat by sweating becomes virtually the only means of maintaining constant temperature. Sweating, by itself, does nothing to cool the body, unless the water is removed by evaporation. High relative humidity retards evaporation.

Selection 17: Recalling Facts

1. Heat is dissipated most effectively by
   □ a. panting.   □ b. perspiration.   □ c. dilation of the arteries.

2. The temperature of the body is controlled by
   □ a. the hypothalamus.   □ b. the cortex.   □ c. the cerebrum.

3. Insensible perspiration
   □ a. cannot be felt.
   □ b. is caused by nervousness.
   □ c. indicates illness.

4. What percentage of body heat is dissipated by the skin?
   □ a. 30 percent   □ b. 60 percent   □ c. 90 percent

5. Which one of the following animals is warm-blooded?
   □ a. A snake   □ b. A fish   □ c. A bird

Selection 17: Understanding Ideas

6. According to the author, warm-blooded animals
   □ a. maintain a constant body temperature.
   □ b. have body temperatures above 98 degrees.
   □ c. prefer warm climates.

7. Sweating will lower the body's temperature if
   □ a. a person is at rest.
   □ b. the heart pumps faster.
   □ c. relative humidity is low.

8. This article is concerned primarily with
   □ a. physical fitness through exercise.
   □ b. the regulatory functions of the brain.
   □ c. the body's ability to survive extreme temperatures.

9. The circulatory system loses its ability to cool the body when
   □ a. environmental temperatures approach 100 degrees.
   □ b. breathing is restricted.
   □ c. clothing is too tight.

10. We can conclude that
    □ a. the body is a sensitive mechanism.
    □ b. most warm-blooded animals cannot survive high temperatures.
    □ c. exercise can increase the heart's ability to pump blood.

18. Pollution Problems

Reading Time _____

Comprehension Score _____

Words per Minute _____

The water that flows into a lake or from a river into the ocean reflects everything that happens on the land within the drainage basin, or watershed, of that lake or river. Correction of a pollution problem in a river must, therefore, consist of an integrated approach that will include corrective measures for all sources within the river basin.

Most river basins contain large areas of agricultural lands. The degree of pollution from livestock and agricultural chemicals will vary in different parts of the country according to the type of agriculture being practiced. Contamination of waters by industry will also depend upon the types of industry located within the basin as well as upon the degree of industrial development.

Urban pollution, primarily from sewage disposal, will vary with population distribution and concentration and the degree of effective sewage treatment.

Water problems in the future will become more intense and more complex. Our increasing population will tremendously increase urban wastes, primarily sewage. On the other hand, increasing demands for water will decrease substantially the amount of water available for diluting wastes. Rapidly expanding industries which involve more and more complex chemical processes will produce larger volumes of effluents, and many of these will contain chemicals which are either toxic or noxious. To feed our rapidly expanding population, agriculture will have to be intensified. This will involve ever-increasing quantities of agricultural chemicals. From this, it is apparent that drastic steps must be taken immediately to develop corrective measures for the pollution problem.

There are two ways by which this pollution problem can be mitigated. The first relates to the treatment of wastes to decrease their pollution hazard. This involves the processing of solid wastes prior to disposal and the treatment of liquid wastes, or effluents, to permit the reuse of the water or minimize pollution upon final disposal.

A second approach is to develop an economic use for all or a part of the wastes. Farm manure is spread in fields as a nutrient and organic supplement. Effluents from sewage disposal plants are used in some areas both for irrigation and for the nutrients contained. Effluents from other processing plants may also be used as a supplemental source of water. Many industries, such as meat and poultry processing plants, are currently converting former waste products into marketable byproducts. Other industries are exploring potential economic uses for their waste products.

Selection 18: Recalling Facts

1. Most river basins contain large areas of land which is
   - ☐ a. agricultural.
   - ☐ b. commercial.
   - ☐ c. residential.

2. Water problems in the future will be
   - ☐ a. less severe.
   - ☐ b. eliminated.
   - ☐ c. more complex.

3. Effluents are being used in some areas as
   - ☐ a. inexpensive fuel.
   - ☐ b. animal feed.
   - ☐ c. supplemental irrigation.

4. A primary source of urban pollution is
   - ☐ a. garbage.
   - ☐ b. detergents.
   - ☐ c. sewage.

5. How many solutions to the water pollution problem are offered?
   - ☐ a. Two
   - ☐ b. Three
   - ☐ c. Four

Selection 18: Understanding Ideas

6. The purpose of this selection is
   - ☐ a. to acquaint the reader with water pollution problems.
   - ☐ b. to alert the reader to the dwindling water supply.
   - ☐ c. to explain industrial uses of water.

7. The author implies that correcting a pollution problem in a river
   - ☐ a. can be a dangerous job.
   - ☐ b. necessitates a survey of land areas.
   - ☐ c. requires a careful study of underwater plant growth.

8. This selection could be labeled
   - ☐ a. argumentation.
   - ☐ b. exposition.
   - ☐ c. narration.

9. The author gives substance to the selection through the use of
   - ☐ a. interviews with authorities in the field of water controls.
   - ☐ b. definitions which clarify important terms.
   - ☐ c. opinions and personal observations.

10. The reader can conclude that
    - ☐ a. some industries are now making economic use of wastes.
    - ☐ b. countries of the world will work together on pollution problems.
    - ☐ c. science is making great progress on increasing water supplies.

19. The Insect Hordes

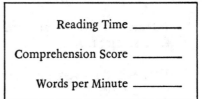

Reading Time ⎯⎯⎯⎯

Comprehension Score ⎯⎯⎯⎯

Words per Minute ⎯⎯⎯⎯

Insects are man's greatest competitor for food and fiber. They are the transmitters of such ancient pestilences as malaria, sleeping sickness, yellow fever, and bubonic plague. These threats to our public health and agricultural abundance are held in check only through the determination of the entomologist and the versatility of the organic chemist.

A major breakthrough in the development of organic pesticides was the discovery and application of DDT in 1939. So effective was DDT in early studies that many predicted the eventual eradication of several insect species. However, they did not reckon with the ability of insects to develop resistance.

Undaunted, the organic chemists proceeded to synthesize the chemical relatives of DDT and other chemicals, some of which were even more toxic to insects than DDT. Toxicants were discovered which provided the farmer and the public health official with undreamed of weapons against the insect hordes. Inexorably, however, the insects retaliated with their extensive capacity to evolve strains resistant to most or all insecticides. Recently, the development of more precise and sensitive methods of analysis for pesticide residues has revealed a disturbing persistence of some of these chemicals in our environment.

Most pesticides are not only toxic to insects, but also to other animals and man. Concern about our environmental health and wildlife and the problem of increasing insecticide resistance requires a new approach to insect control. The agricultural and health demands of our society will not permit a return to methods of control used before 1959. Thus, more fundamental approaches to insect control must be found. The biological, biochemical, and behavioral differences which set insects apart from other animals must be sought after and understood. A study of insect life, feeding, growth, development, and reproduction must be made in order to understand the fundamental differences between insects and other animals. Such a study will permit the development of selective tools for insect control uncomplicated by eventual insect resistance and the potential hazard to human populations.

One such approach to insect control is the application of our rapidly expanding knowledge of how insects rely upon hormones to regulate their growth, feeding, mating, reproduction, and diapause—a state akin to hibernation. Experimental tampering with the hormone-producing machinery can cause an immature insect to stop developing, or to grow too fast. Most of these effects result in the insect's premature death.

Selection 19: Recalling Facts

1. Insects can infect man with
   □ a. scarlet fever.   □ b. pneumonia.   □ c. malaria.

2. DDT was discovered in the late
   □ a. 1920s.   □ b. 1930s.   □ c. 1940s.

3. DDT is described as
   □ a. an organic pesticide.   □ b. an inert pesticide.   □ c. a synthetic pesticide.

4. According to the author, DDT is a
   □ a. hormone regulator.   □ b. toxic substance.   □ c. biochemical stabilizer.

5. So effective was DDT in early studies that some scientists predicted
   □ a. eventual eradication of several insect species.
   □ b. increased importance of organic gardening.
   □ c. future dissatisfaction with natural fertilizers.

Selection 19: Understanding Ideas

6. The author feels that the best way to control insects is with
   □ a. biochemical warfare.
   □ b. hormone stimulators.
   □ c. synthetic compounds.

7. One drawback to the use of DDT is that
   □ a. it does not dissolve readily.
   □ b. it loses its lethal qualities soon after it is applied.
   □ c. it leaves a harmful residue.

8. According to the article, an entomologist studies
   □ a. diseases.   □ b. insects.   □ c. farming techniques.

9. The reader can assume that
   □ a. DDT is the strongest insecticide made.
   □ b. several insecticides are similar to DDT in their chemical structures.
   □ c. the formula for DDT was discovered by accident.

10. Scientists who first studied DDT did not anticipate that
    □ a. it would kill many varieties of plants.
    □ b. it would pollute the atmosphere.
    □ c. many insects would become immune to it.

20. Man Versus Machine

Reading Time _____

Comprehension Score _____

Words per Minute _____

Vegetable crops have been and continue to be enormous users of hand labor. Until recently, these crops have resisted the trend toward mechanization. Although some of the cultural, postharvest, and marketing practices of vegetable growers are among the most modern in present-day agriculture, vegetable thinning and harvesting operations do not differ essentially from those used in the 1920s and 1930s.

This picture is now changing rapidly. The scarcity and cost of hand labor are creating pressures that have accelerated the trend toward mechanization in vegetable production. There seems little doubt that those vegetable crops produced in large volume will soon be fully mechanized. The processing tomato in California is a good example of a crop where the harvest has been almost completely mechanized within a period of less than ten years. Rapid progress in mechanical harvesting of this crop must be credited to the close cooperation of plant breeder and mechanical engineer.

Designing plants for complete mechanization has presented the plant breeder with a challenging array of new and exciting problems. The problems of each crop demand somewhat different solutions.

In lettuce, for example, it may not be necessary to alter present-day varieties drastically to make them suitable for mechanization, although varieties with an upright frame and with the lower leaves a half inch to an inch above the soil are likely to be preferred to those having leaves flush with the soil. Lettuce is self-pollinated, and usually the percentage of out-crossing is low. Therefore, we find great genetic uniformity in this crop.

If we assume that the commonly used varieties of lettuce are genetically uniform, further uniformity in growth and development must come from improved cultural practices. In other words, the grower must create a more favorable environment for planting, germination, and development of the plant. Proper bed design and precision planting of high-quality seed are essential for mechanization. Usually in conventional planting, an excess of seed is used, and the plants are hand thinned to the desired spacing. This procedure is wasteful of seed and requires costly hand labor.

But an even more serious defect of overplanting is that it favors uneven plant growth because of crowding, competition, and mechanical injury to the young seedlings from which they never completely recover.

The ideal is to plant one seed or one mature lettuce plant at the desired spacing.

Selection 20: Recalling Facts

1. The growing and harvest of which vegetable has been almost completely mechanized?
   □ a. Potatoes   □ b. Tomatoes   □ c. Peppers

2. Mechanized vegetable production has been in operation for nearly
   □ a. five years.   □ b. ten years.   □ c. twenty years.

3. For mechanized farming, the farmer must
   □ a. select seeds carefully.
   □ b. use a potassium fertilizer.
   □ c. mix sand with soil.

4. A farmer who follows conventional planting methods
   □ a. wastes seeds.
   □ b. uses organic fertilizers.
   □ c. plants his crops after the last full moon of winter.

5. In this article, the author mentions the state of
   □ a. Oregon.   □ b. Idaho.   □ c. California.

Selection 20: Understanding Ideas

6. The acceleration of mechanized harvesting has been caused by
   □ a. population growth.   □ b. unemployment.   □ c. increasing labor costs.

7. Lettuce is an example of a plant
   □ a. that is difficult to crossbreed.
   □ b. that will not adapt well to mechanization.
   □ c. that shows genetic uniformity.

8. Compared to hand labor, mechanization of crop production today is
   □ a. time consuming.   □ b. less acceptable.   □ c. less costly.

9. According to the author, overplanting often produces
   □ a. inferior plants.
   □ b. a wide variety of hybrids.
   □ c. self-pollinating plants.

10. Much of the responsibility for successful mechanization lies with
    □ a. the manufacturer of specialized equipment.
    □ b. the federal government.
    □ c. community zoning boards.

21. Youth Service Programs

Reading Time _____

Comprehension Score _____

Words per Minute _____

Communities seriously interested in securing greater justice for youth should establish, or expand, a network of legal services in the juvenile justice system. To be effective, these services should range from the point of arrest through the time of release from parole. The advocacy role of the lawyer should be broad enough not only to represent his client's interests in the technical legal sense, but also to speak out for alternative means of handling cases. Moreover, he should be able to suggest to policy makers new programs and services which need to be created.

Many experts believe that such legal services programs can most effectively be carried out under the auspices of private agencies rather than under the aegis of the courts and correctional agencies. Support for these programs, in any case, would most likely have to come from public funds.

What may be said for legal service programs may also be said for social work community organization programs. Community organization workers can examine areas of neglect and point up the need for new youth services. They can also be used to muster public support for the development of these services.

The influence of community organization programs can also serve to enlist the support and develop the confidence of the poor in the juvenile justice system. Today, police, courts, and correctional agencies that lack sustaining relationships with ghetto communities, youth, and other citizens are in imminent danger of becoming progressively isolated from, and sharply criticized by, these groups.

As with legal service programs, community organization activity might best be based in nongovernmental agencies under the direction of representative citizen groups. So situated and so based, programs of this type can more effectively criticize, where necessary, existing practices and introduce what many consider to be long overdue changes.

Such organizations might act as mediators between different groups engaged in social conflict and public disputes. There is a pressing need for some agency or group, having the confidence of the various sides, to mediate effective resolutions to the many conflicts which beset our society today on the college campuses, the ghettos, and other settings.

Realistically, it must be noted that some of these disputes are not likely to yield easily, or at all, to even the best mediation efforts. But the significant point to be made is that the lack of such services represents a serious program gap in most communities at the present time.

Selection 21: Recalling Facts

1. Legal services for youth should extend from
   ☐ a. conviction to jail.   ☐ b. trial to sentencing.   ☐ c. arrest to release.

2. The role of the lawyer should be
   ☐ a. strengthened.   ☐ b. broadened.   ☐ c. narrowed.

3. Legal service programs should be carried out by
   ☐ a. court systems.   ☐ b. private agencies.   ☐ c. correctional agencies.

4. Financing for new legal service programs would have to come from
   ☐ a. government funds.   ☐ b. private agencies.   ☐ c. correctional agencies.

5. Police courts which lack lasting relationships with ghettos risk
   ☐ a. isolation.   ☐ b. violence.   ☐ c. bankruptcy.

Selection 21: Understanding Ideas

6. The author recommends that legal service programs be run by
   ☐ a. the Department of Justice.
   ☐ b. governors' councils in each of the fifty states.
   ☐ c. community residents who are concerned with the program.

7. A serious program gap exists in most communities in the area of
   ☐ a. bringing antagonistic parties together to resolve issues.
   ☐ b. examining low-income housing in high crime areas.
   ☐ c. financing health-oriented programs for youth.

8. To develop his point, the author uses
   ☐ a. common-sense knowledge.
   ☐ b. documented proof.
   ☐ c. personal beliefs.

9. The author's position
   ☐ a. seems realistic.
   ☐ b. appears naive.
   ☐ c. is oversimplified.

10. The main thought of this selection is that
    ☐ a. communities should provide legal services to juveniles.
    ☐ b. the legal profession should treat all cases fairly.
    ☐ c. the American legal system should be overhauled.

22. Unlucky Strikes

During the past forty years, cancer of the lung in the United States has shown the greatest increase of any cancer type. Compared to 3,000 deaths from lung cancer in 1930, the number of deaths is expected to rise to 84,000 in 1981. If the present trend continues, it is estimated that about one million persons who are now school children will die eventually of lung cancer.

Such an alarming increase assumes the proportions of an epidemic. At least 70 percent of the total increase can be attributed to cigarette smoking. An additional factor is air pollution caused by industrial wastes, automobile exhausts and household sources.

The first studies on the relationship of smoking to lung cancer were of patients with the disease who were asked about their smoking habits. Their answers were compared with those of noncancer patients. Almost all lung cancer patients replied that they had been long-term, heavy cigarette smokers.

The next studies were of large groups of men who were first identified by their smoking habits, then were followed for several years. Deaths from all causes increased among smokers according to the amount smoked. But the most striking proportional rise was in deaths from lung cancer.

While these clues were being obtained from population studies, scientists began to study the smoking and cancer relationship in the laboratory. Chemists isolated and identified at least a dozen carcinogenic chemicals of the hydrocarbon type in the tars from tobacco smoke. There is evidence that tobacco smoke contains yet further carcinogens.

The membranes lining the lungs absorb cancer-producing chemicals from tobacco smoke. The protective mechanisms by which the lungs rid themselves of impurities are first paralyzed and then destroyed by tobacco smoke. Prolonged exposure of animals to tobacco smoke produces changes in cells that resemble early stages of cancer development. These changes are also seen in the lungs of heavy smokers who die of causes other than lung cancer.

Health hazards of smoking are not limited to lung cancer. Bronchitis, emphysema and other crippling lung diseases are produced in even larger numbers. Deaths from heart disease are accelerated and increased. While cigarette smoking is a major cause of lung cancer, other uses of tobacco are associated with cancers of the oral cavity among cigar smokers and cancers of the lip among pipe smokers.

Selection 22: Recalling Facts

1. In the U.S. the incidence of lung cancer has shown the greatest increase
   □ a. during the past 20 years.
   □ b. during the past 30 years.
   □ c. during the past 40 years.

2. What percentage of the increase in cases of lung cancer can be traced to smoking?
   □ a. 30 percent   □ b. 50 percent   □ c. 70 percent

3. In the 1930s cancer annually claimed
   □ a. 3,000 lives.   □ b. 10,000 lives.   □ c. 26,000 lives.

4. A substance in tobacco that the author mentions is
   □ a. nicotine.   □ b. tar.   □ c. carbon.

5. Cancer of the mouth has been traced to
   □ a. cigarette smoking.   □ b. pipe smoking.   □ c. cigar smoking.

Selection 22: Understanding Ideas

6. A factor which has increased the incidence of lung cancer is
   □ a. the use of preservatives in food.
   □ b. the lack of concern for adequate exercise.
   □ c. the increase in levels of pollution.

7. According to the author, carcinogenics
   □ a. are used to treat cancer.
   □ b. are natural hormones in the human body.
   □ c. are harmful substances that cause cancer.

8. Smoking directly affects
   □ a. the action of the heart.
   □ b. the functions of the large intestine.
   □ c. the circulation of blood in the legs.

9. A disease that is more common than lung cancer is
   □ a. emphysema.   □ b. leukemia.   □ c. diabetes.

10. The reader can conclude that
    □ a. smoking increases the body's need for vitamin E.
    □ b. smoking increases the risk of contracting a number of diseases.
    □ c. smoking increases the desire for high-calorie foods.

23. Land at Any Price

Land is many things. It is space to park a car, a place to build a patio, or the site for an office building. On a Sunday drive, it is a view, a roadside park, or a hiking trail.

But only three percent of the total land area of the 48 contiguous states is taken up by cities, industry, highways, and similar uses. About three-fifths is used for crops and livestock production. The 1.1 billion acres in farms, including the buildings, had a market value of nearly $200 billion in early 1968. Such rural lands account for nearly a fourth of all taxable real estate outside our major cities.

There are many variables at work in the determination of land values. How it is used and how well it suits its purpose are two of the leading price factors.

Land can be priced by the square foot, by the acre, or by the square mile. A square foot located on a choice corner in Manhattan, New York City, may be priced at $200; in Manhattan, Kansas, perhaps $1; and in Illinois corn country, one or two cents. There are 43,560 square feet in an acre. Up to 25,000 corn plants can be grown on one acre. The land for each plant would cost a nickel and produce about six ounces of corn.

The desert country of Arizona, our sixth largest state in land area, is priced by the section. One section equals one square mile or 640 acres. The cost of land in this area of the country averages a tenth of a cent for each square foot. But even ten square miles would represent just a modest cattle spread. It would provide grass for only 300 to 400 cattle.

If this block of land were laid out in one-, two-, or five-acre plots and if a water system, roads, a shopping center, a golf course, and a recreation center were built, the original desert would become a new commodity.

California has the widest range in land prices of any state. Topping the list for agricultural uses are avocado groves, about $7,000 an acre. Citrus groves in the path of subdivisions may bring even more. Irrigated lands suitable for cotton and vegetables carry price tags of $1,000 to $1,500 an acre.

Rangeland in the northern part ot the state is more likely to be priced according to the amount of forage produced than by the acre. Eight hundred dollars worth of land to provide for one animal would be typical.

Selection 23: Recalling Facts

1. How much of the total available land is used for farming in the United States?
   ☐ a. One-fifth   ☐ b. One-half   ☐ c. Three-fifths

2. Approximately how much land is contained in an acre?
   ☐ a. 20,000 square feet   ☐ b. 40,000 square feet   ☐ c. 60,000 square feet

3. Ten square miles of land provides enough grass for a maximum of
   ☐ a. 200 cattle.   ☐ b. 400 cattle.   ☐ c. 800 cattle.

4. The widest range of land prices in any state can be found in
   ☐ a. Texas.   ☐ b. Nevada.   ☐ c. California.

5. The most expensive agricultural land is used to grow
   ☐ a. oranges.   ☐ b. grapes.   ☐ c. avocados.

Selection 23: Understanding Ideas

6. The author implies that the most expensive land is located in
   ☐ a. Dallas.   ☐ b. Los Angeles.   ☐ c. New York City.

7. The article suggests that the least expensive land
   ☐ a. is found in New England.
   ☐ b. is utilized for farming.
   ☐ c. is often taxed excessively.

8. Desert areas are usually bought by the section because
   ☐ a. large amounts are bought at one time.
   ☐ b. desert land has no real value.
   ☐ c. desert land is subdivided after it is purchased.

9. According to the article, subdividing land
   ☐ a. reduces taxes.
   ☐ b. increases value.
   ☐ c. improves drainage.

10. We can conclude that
    ☐ a. virgin land is more valuable than developed land.
    ☐ b. land is taxed according to use and location.
    ☐ c. church property is not usually taxed.

24. More Rare Than Rubies

There was a time when the word "prospector" conjured up visions of whiskery desert rats toting pickaxes and shambling with their mules out of a thousand Western novels toward a thousand cinematic sunsets.

No more. Prospecting has joined the space age. It hasn't happened in a flash. Over the years, mineral companies have analyzed water flowing in mountain streams for clues to ore bodies. Electrical and magnetic prospecting devices used in combination with geochemical analyses and field studies have led the mineral industry to a variety of ore deposits.

Recent changes have been toward greater sophistication. Today's tools are infrared cameras and mercury vapor detectors, computers and helicopters. And in addition, modern prospectors scrutinize the treetops, study sound waves and observe plant life.

What's behind the transformation? It all began as a kind of scientific detective case. The culprit in this caper was technological society. Like a glutton on a binge, it was eating up the rare heavy metals—tin, antimony, mercury, bismuth, nickel, tantalum, platinum, silver, gold. With precious reserves dwindling ominously, the U.S. Geological Survey, an arm of the Department of the Interior, began field-testing techniques that may aid in uncovering additional mineral resources.

The government acted because these rare metals are vitally necessary to sophisticated 20th century technology. Each of them has a long list of uses, and many of them are absolutely indispensable.

Nickel is added to steel wherever great strength and corrosion resistance are needed. Mercury, used in scientific apparatus, is also vital to the electronics industry for such components as rectifiers and switches.

Platinum, too, is used in electronics (for contact points), while tin goes into such important products as solder. Antimony plays a part in rubber production, and gold and silver aren't limited to baubles.

Photography depends on silver compounds, and the U.S. alone annually consumes over thirty million ounces of silver for electronic parts like telephone relays.

Without gold (for semiconductors, connectors, printed circuits), computers wouldn't think so fast. A shortage of these metals, and others like them, would create a serious problem for society.

For the Survey's geologist-sleuths, it was a tough assignment: how to track down new deposits of the vital metals? By now, few ore deposits marked by surface outcrops are undiscovered. The deposits that space-age prospectors have to search out are hidden under tons of rock and earth.

Selection 24: Recalling Facts

1. The U.S. Geological Survey is a branch of which government department?
   □ a. Agriculture □ b. Commerce □ c. Interior

2. The metal added to steel for greater strength is
   □ a. nickel. □ b. platinum. □ c. bismuth.

3. The electronics industry is greatly dependent upon
   □ a. nickel. □ b. mercury. □ c. antimony.

4. How many ounces of silver does the U.S. consume annually for electronics?
   □ a. 10 million □ b. 20 million □ c. 30 million

5. Who initiated a drive to ensure continued supplies of rare metals?
   □ a. Mineral companies □ b. The government □ c. Electronics companies

Selection 24: Understanding Ideas

6. This article is primarily about
   □ a. the mining of precious metals.
   □ b. prospecting for precious metals.
   □ c. the need for precious metals.

7. The phrase, "like a glutton on a binge, it was eating up . . . metals" is
   □ a. literal language.
   □ b. figurative language.
   □ c. scientific description.

8. The function of the U.S. Geological Survey is
   □ a. to uncover new sources of minerals.
   □ b. to develop new laboratory technology to conserve rare metals.
   □ c. to find territory which has never been explored for minerals.

9. The author implies that gold and silver are used
   □ a. primarily by the jewelry industry.
   □ b. in the manufacture of many products.
   □ c. in smaller quantitites than other metals.

10. We can conclude that
    □ a. new sources of heavy metals will be found.
    □ b. used metals must be recycled if supplies are to last.
    □ c. industry must find substitute metals which are more common.

25. An Idea and an Institution

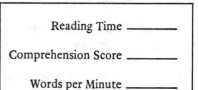

The U.S. National Arboretum is an oasis of 415 acres of nature's beauty that is bounded by the Anacostia River, the Baltimore Parkway, and the business activities of the northeast section of Washington, D.C. Established by Congress in 1927, its major purpose is to provide information on the landscape.

Visitors can enjoy an array of ordered beauty, skillfully arranged in a pleasing setting of woodland and meadow. This beauty, within reach of every citizen, is made up of native trees indigenous to the northeastern United States, the exotic plants from plant explorations, demonstration plantings, and the nature walks through flowering azaleas, woodland herbs, and grassy meadows.

A stroll through the dwarf conifers collection at the Arboretum strikes the visitor with deep impressions of solitude. Here the conifers of normal growth contrast pleasingly with their dwarf counterparts, in an arrangement of rocks and stone-mulched beds, set among velvet-green grass walkways.

The President has called upon all of us to look at our surroundings and to determine what can be made beautiful, or more beautiful, or even what should be removed for the sake of beauty. Beauty now comes to have special meaning to us. How can such a plea be translated into reality? How can the many communities in our nation find answers to the implications of such a task?

Destiny has brought an idea and an institution together. Fulfillment of the ideal of beauty is now made possible by the existence of this great horticultural center, the National Arboretum, which is a mecca for those in search of beauty. It is a meeting place for the teachers, professionals, and laymen with horticultural interests.

The National Arboretum, with its staff of ornamental horticulturists and botanists, endeavors to present to the public—through its exhibition plantings, gardens, and demonstration plots—the essentials of beautification.

Literature on plant subjects illustrating new plants, planting techniques, and landscape schemes is provided through an active publication series. The lecture series and the formalized courses of the National Arboretum provide the student with technical knowledge and open new avenues of thought. Plant explorations are carried on with the Agricultural Research Service. Such explorations across the world lead to discovery of exotic plants that might be suitable for landscape use in our own nation.

With its research programs, the National Arboretum is making both inspirational and tangible contributions to the national beautification program.

Selection 25: Recalling Facts

1. The National Arboretum is situated on more than
   - ☐ a. 400 acres.
   - ☐ b. 500 acres.
   - ☐ c. 600 acres.

2. The Arboretum displays a dwarf variety of
   - ☐ a. broadleafs.
   - ☐ b. conifers.
   - ☐ c. bonsai.

3. The author refers to the National Arboretum as
   - ☐ a. a mecca.
   - ☐ b. an isthmus.
   - ☐ c. a delta.

4. According to the article, the Arboretum staff includes
   - ☐ a. psychologists.
   - ☐ b. botanists.
   - ☐ c. zoologists.

5. The National Arboretum is located in
   - ☐ a. Chicago.
   - ☐ b. Los Angeles.
   - ☐ c. Baltimore.

Selection 25: Understanding Ideas

6. This article is primarily about
   - ☐ a. research programs of the National Arboretum.
   - ☐ b. tropical plants in American aboretums.
   - ☐ c. the functions of the country's largest arboretum.

7. The National Arboretum keeps interest in natural beauty alive through
   - ☐ a. a lecturer exchange agreement with foreign countries.
   - ☐ b. a plant loan program with colleges and universities.
   - ☐ c. a number of publications about nature.

8. The primary function of arboretums is
   - ☐ a. to display rare plant forms.
   - ☐ b. to provide information about the landscape.
   - ☐ c. to encourage research in the causes of pollution.

9. From this article, the reader can assume that
   - ☐ a. foreign plants can adapt themselves to new environments.
   - ☐ b. arboretums are federally sponsored projects.
   - ☐ c. azaleas are difficult to crossbreed.

10. The article implies that the National Arboretum resulted from
    - ☐ a. a rising tide of concern over polluted water.
    - ☐ b. a presidential plea to beautify the environment.
    - ☐ c. a local businessman's love of nature.

26. Finding Gold

Reading Time _____

Comprehension Score _____

Words per Minute _____

Gold can be found in many different kinds of rock and in many geological environments. It is often found with other metals. In fact, more than one-third of the gold produced in the United States is a byproduct from mining other metallic ores. Where base metals are deposited, either in veins or as scattered mineral grains, minor amounts of gold are usually deposited with them. Deposits of this type are mined for the predominant metals, but during processing of the ore, the gold is also recovered.

Some deposits of base metals are so large that even though they contain only a small amount of gold per ton, so much is mined that a substantial amount of gold is recovered. Gold recovered from copper ore mined at the vast open-pit mine at Bingham, Utah, for example, almost equals the amount of gold produced from the largest gold mine in the United States.

Geologists study all the factors that control the origin and emplacement of mineral deposits, including gold. Studies of igneous rocks in the field and in the laboratory lead to an understanding of how they came to their present location, how they crystallized to solid rock, and how mineral-bearing solutions and gases formed within them. Studies of rock structures, such as folds, faults, fractures, and joints, and of the effects of heat and pressure on rocks suggest why and where fracturing of the crust took place and where veins might be found. Knowledge of the physical and chemical characteristics of rocks yields information on the pattern of fractures and where to look for them. Studies of weathering processes and transport of material by water enable geologists to predict the most likely places for placer deposits to form.

Research on prospecting methods has led to the development of chemical and spectrographic laboratories that are fitted with newly designed analytical instruments capable of detecting and rapidly measuring the amounts of gold and other valuable metals that may be present in the rocks and ores. These laboratories can accompany the geologist into the field and, by providing on-the-spot analyses of selected samples, guide the geologist in his search.

The occurrence of gold is not capricious; its presence in various kinds of rocks and formation under differing environmental conditions follow natural laws. As geologists increase their knowledge of the ore-forming processes they can expect to improve their ability to find gold.

Selection 26: Recalling Facts

1. What fraction of U.S. gold is a byproduct from mining other ores?
   ☐ a. One-fourth   ☐ b. One-third   ☐ c. One-half

2. The U.S. has a large open-pit copper mine in
   ☐ a. Alabama.   ☐ b. Mississippi.   ☐ c. Utah.

3. What type of rock formations reveals the origins of other rocks?
   ☐ a. Igneous   ☐ b. Extrusive   ☐ c. Plutonic

4. The occurrence of gold is not
   ☐ a. common.   ☐ b. capricious.   ☐ c. geological.

5. Geologists are trying to improve their ability to
   ☐ a. find gold.   ☐ b. refine metals.   ☐ c. understand minerals.

Selection 26: Understanding Ideas

6. The author suggests that
   ☐ a. the occurrence of gold does not follow natural laws.
   ☐ b. the quality of base metal is improved if it is near gold.
   ☐ c. heat and pressure have a great effect on creating minerals.

7. Geologists limit their study to
   ☐ a. the prediction of base metal content in ore.
   ☐ b. the development of gold recovery techniques.
   ☐ c. the origins and locations of mineral deposits.

8. Spectrographic laboratories
   ☐ a. record faults and fractures as they occur.
   ☐ b. study weathering processes which affect mineral formations.
   ☐ c. measure the amount of precious metals in base ore.

9. Spectrographic laboratories are really
   ☐ a. mobile units for work in the field.
   ☐ b. massive structures of complicated technology.
   ☐ c. branch laboratories of colleges and universities.

10. We can conclude from this selection that
    ☐ a. most smelting plants are equipped to recover gold.
    ☐ b. many people do not recognize gold when they see it.
    ☐ c. much gold is lost in inefficient mining operations.

27. Conservation

One basic concept of a classical conservation philosophy is identity of uniqueness in the natural environment. Proper application of this concept includes biological and geological resources—both renewable and nonrenewable.

The establishment of Yellowstone Park a century ago was the first national step implementing the concept. Here, a major land area was set aside in order to preserve unique natural features for the education and enjoyment of all people. The park has been protected in spite of great resource values known to exist within its boundaries such as gold, hydropower, and geothermal energy. The Everglades National Park is a similar preserve where visitors can enjoy a rare and delicate ecosystem peculiar to a subtropical, water-based ecology in its natural state. Other areas, such as the Alaska Wildlife Refuge, are protected and exempted even from the kind of access permitted in national parks. The federal government has set aside national parks, national monuments, and wildlife refuges. A wilderness system is currently in progress.

In like fashion mineral resource areas can be truly unique in their character and in their occurrence in the accessible part of the earth's crust. Famous mineral districts like Butte, Montana; Bingham Canyon, Utah; Lead, South Dakota, are rare occurrences on a planetary basis. Unlike the unique vistas and wildlife domains, unusual mineral deposits serve the public good if they are recovered in a systematic way. In the long history of man, exploration and development of mineral resources at specific sites have been temporary operations. With proper planning before extraction is begun and proper restoration of the terrain after extraction, there need be little adverse environmental impact in acceptable tradeoff of resource values and multiple use of the total resource base.

The concept of multiple use and sustained yield were two guiding principles of the classical conservation philosophy expressed at the turn of the century. Conflicting uses and permanent damage to other potential resource values have been elements of recent debate and will remain as important subjects in a pluralistic society which requires both renewable and nonrenewable resources to maintain its health, welfare, and vigor. It is understandable now that economic values received highest priority during the developmental stage of our society. Today the American society is mature in an economic sense. Understandable pressures are increasing to preserve our dwindling acreage of the natural terrain, particularly on the public lands.

Selection 27: Recalling Facts

1. The Everglades National Park is an example of
   - □ a. a water-based ecology.
   - □ b. a nonrenewable resource.
   - □ c. a temporary environment.

2. The author mentions mineral districts in
   - □ a. the West. □ b. the South. □ c. the East.

3. Mineral deposits should be recovered
   - □ a. periodically. □ b. regionally. □ c. systematically.

4. The concept of multiple use and sustained yield go back to
   - □ a. 1900. □ b. 1920. □ c. 1950.

5. The author feels that in an economic sense the American society is
   - □ a. unrealistic. □ b. childish. □ c. mature.

Selection 27: Understanding Ideas

6. The park with the tightest restrictions is
   - □ a. Yellowstone Park.
   - □ b. Everglades National Park.
   - □ c. the Alaska Wildlife Refuge.

7. The author leads the reader to believe that
   - □ a. biological and geological resources are not renewable.
   - □ b. national parks contain many untapped natural resources.
   - □ c. terrain cannot be restored after mineral extraction.

8. To make his point clear, the author uses
   - □ a. the technique of comparison and contrast.
   - □ b. personal opinions supported by observable facts.
   - □ c. simple chronological order of events.

9. Butte, Bingham Canyon, and Lead are mentioned as examples of
   - □ a. famous wildlife domains.
   - □ b. delicate ecosystems.
   - □ c. areas of superior mineral deposits.

10. The author feels that adverse environmental impact in mining
   - □ a. is a fact of life which is evident in every country.
   - □ b. illustrates an indifferent attitude toward the landscape.
   - □ c. can be avoided through proper planning and restoration.

28. The Drinker's Dilemma

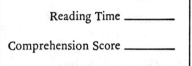

Reading Time _____

Comprehension Score _____

Words per Minute _____

Prolonged and excessive use of alcohol can seriously undermine an individual's health. Physical deterioration occurs because large quantities of alcohol can directly damage body tissue and indirectly cause malnutrition. Nutritional deficiencies can result for several reasons. Alcohol contains empty calories, which have no significant nutritive value. When consumed in substantial amounts, alcohol curbs one's appetite for more wholesome foods. Excessive alcohol intake can interfere with the proper digestion and absorption of food. Therefore, even the heavy drinker who does eat a well-balanced diet is deprived of some essential nutrients. Maintenance of a drinking habit can deplete economic resources otherwise available for buying good, wholesome food. Malnutrition itself further reduces the body's ability to utilize the nutrients consumed. The results of damaged tissue and malnutrition can be brain injury, heart disease, diabetes, ulcers, cirrhosis or cancer of the liver, and weakened muscle tissue. Untreated alcoholism can reduce one's life span by ten to twelve years.

Heavy alcohol consumption also affects the body's usage of other drugs and medications. The dosages required by excessive drinkers may differ from those required by normal or non-drinkers. Serious consequences can be incurred unless the prescribing physician is aware of the patient's drinking habits.

Sudden death may result from excessive drinking. It might occur when the individual has ingested such a large amount of alcohol that the brain center controlling breathing and heart action is adversely affected, or when taking some other drugs, particularly sleep preparations, along with alcohol. Death, as a result of excessive drinking, can come during an automobile accident since half of all fatal traffic accidents involve the use of alcohol. Many self-inflicted deaths, as well as homicides, involve the use of alcohol.

It is important to remember that alcohol is a drug that is potentially addictive. Once the user is hooked on alcohol, withdrawal symptoms occur when it is not sufficiently available to body cells. At the onset of developing alcohol addiction, these symptoms may be relatively mild and include hand tremors, anxiety, nausea, and sweating. As dependency increases, so does the severity of the withdrawal syndrome and the need for medical assistance to cope with it.

In 1956 the American Medical Association supported the growing acceptance of alcoholism as an illness, falling under the treatment jurisdiction of the medical profession. Since then, the medical resources for problems of acute and chronic intoxication have increased and improved.

Selection 28: Recalling Facts

1. Untreated alcoholism can reduce a person's life by
   □ a. 5 years.   □ b. 12 years.   □ c. 22 years.

2. The article points out that heavy drinking can cause
   □ a. arthritis.   □ b. muscle debility.   □ c. blindness.

3. What fraction of all fatal traffic accidents results from the abuse of alcohol?
   □ a. One-quarter   □ b. One-half   □ c. Two-thirds

4. The author refers to alcohol as a
   □ a. drug.   □ b. medicinal substance. □ c. high calorie beverage.

5. A heavy drinker suffers from
   □ a. indigestion.   □ b. malnutrition.   □ c. excessive thirst.

Selection 28: Understanding Ideas

6. This selection is concerned mostly with
   □ a. the long-term drinker.
   □ b. the person who drinks on a dare.
   □ c. the person who drinks for the first time.

7. A person who drinks to excess must show caution in
   □ a. having X-rays.
   □ b. engaging in exercise.
   □ c. taking drugs.

8. The author develops a correlation between
   □ a. alcohol use and theft.
   □ b. alcohol absorption and insomnia.
   □ c. alcohol addiction and withdrawal.

9. In the middle 1950s, the American Medical Association
   □ a. proved that alcoholism is an act of free choice.
   □ b. concluded that heredity influenced alcoholism.
   □ c. succumbed to the public acceptance of alcoholism as an illness.

10. To develop his point, the author uses
   □ a. figurative language.
   □ b. scientific facts.
   □ c. convincing arguments.

29. Playing It Safe Abroad

For the great majority of young Americans, travel abroad is a rich and satisfying experience. But for some it has turned out to be a nightmare.

In the last few years, hundreds of young Americans have been sent to foreign jails on drug charges. Many others have been arrested for defrauding banks, merchants, and issuers of traveler's checks. U.S. officials can give only limited assistance to those arrested. Penalties abroad are frequently severe and prison conditions often primitive.

Americans generally are not aware that in some countries many drug pushers are also informers for police or customs officials. Many young Americans learn about this trap the hard way.

Americans mistakenly believe foreign drug law enforcement is less stringent than in the U.S. On the contrary, prosecution of drug offenders has been intensified in countries around the world. Penalties are severe—ranging from six years in jail plus a heavy fine for possession of narcotics up to death in one country. In some countries the sentence is one to three years in a detoxification asylum, a mental hospital. Smoking marijuana can often draw the same penalties as possession or use of heroin.

Besides drugs, there are other hazards the visitor should know about. Private currency transactions with strangers, or street corner deals offering quick profits, can lead to trouble. The traveler should steer clear of black market activities, currency regulation violations, and other illegal dealings. If one is caught, the penalties are severe. Some black market dealers also prove to be police informers. If a visitor is offered an unbelievable bargain, he shouldn't believe it. It may involve stolen goods.

Laws governing cash and traveler's checks are stringent abroad. People who buy at discounts from strangers in the street can spend years in jail regretting a foolish moment. Issuers of traveler's checks, who work with local and international law enforcement authorities, have extensive security arrangements and agents in all countries. Criminal charges range from fraud and forgery to possession of stolen property and counterfeiting.

Some countries restrict purchases of certain luxury items. The visitor should beware of people offering to buy his possessions.

It isn't necessary to leave the country to get involved in the black market. For example, stolen airline tickets, sold at discount to innocent bargain hunters, can get a traveler into big trouble with the law. Airlines now are prosecuting purchasers as well as sellers of stolen tickets. A traveler should make his purchases only at authorized outlets.

Selection 29: Recalling Facts

1. In some countries people are not aware that drug pushers are
    ☐ a. customs officials.   ☐ b. murderers.   ☐ c. informers.

2. The most severe penalty for possession of narcotics is
    ☐ a. 10 years of hard labor.
    ☐ b. 20 years in jail.
    ☐ c. execution.

3. A detoxification asylum is defined in the article as
    ☐ a. a special jail.   ☐ b. a mental hospital.   ☐ c. a sanatorium.

4. Some countries restrict purchases of
    ☐ a. luxury items.   ☐ b. local currencies.   ☐ c. imported goods.

5. Before leaving the U.S., one can be tempted with black market
    ☐ a. luggage.   ☐ b. passports.   ☐ c. airline tickets.

Selection 29: Understanding Ideas

6. This article is primarily about
    ☐ a. getting the best buys with foreign currency.
    ☐ b. planning for a trip abroad.
    ☐ c. using caution in foreign countries.

7. The article suggests that
    ☐ a. smoking marijuana is a serious crime in some countries.
    ☐ b. foreign jails are often filled with Americans.
    ☐ c. traveler's checks are difficult to cash abroad.

8. The author expects that his article will appeal most to
    ☐ a. young people who are studying law.
    ☐ b. people who plan to travel abroad.
    ☐ c. prospective workers in the Peace Corps.

9. For the majority of Americans, traveling abroad is usually
    ☐ a. a gratifying experience.
    ☐ b. a bitter disappointment.
    ☐ c. an expensive proposition.

10. The author bases his ideas on the assumption that
    ☐ a. most foreigners try to cheat Americans.
    ☐ b. Americans are unfamiliar with foreign laws.
    ☐ c. customs officials are difficult to bribe.

30. Buying and Selling

In the course of a person's lifetime, chances are he will buy a home. In fact, he will probably buy and sell several homes. Therefore, he should know something about financing.

Obtaining a mortgage at a reasonable rate of interest can save considerable money over the term of the mortgage.

When one sells, arranging for a value appraisal will give the owner an accurate estimate of the selling price of his home and save valuable time for both himself and the buyer.

During the last four decades, homeownership has become available to most Americans. Prior to 1930, the opportunities for homeownership were scarce. Mortgage loans from private lenders in those days were based solely upon the property as security and did not consider the applicant's ability to repay the loan. The mortgage or short-term note was made for periods extending from two to five years at a specified interest rate.

The lender kept the option of demanding payment in full or renewing the note. If the lender did not choose to refinance the loan at maturity, the mortgagee had to find a new loan, pay off the indebtedness, or lose the property. Individual lenders were the principal source of loans until the disastrous effect of the Depression on real estate and the subsequent demand for housing in the 1940's. Need for expansion and control of credit resulted in the establishment of institutional lending.

In the early 1930s thousands of homeowners were threatened with foreclosure. To stabilize the real estate market, the Homeowners Loan Corporation was organized. Subsequently in 1934, the Federal Housing Administration came into existence.

FHA devised a mortgage whereby real estate loans could be made on a long-term basis rather than the customary two to five years. Such loans provided for regular monthly installments which included real estate taxes and insurance. To do this on a sound basis, a uniform system of real estate appraisal and credit analysis of the borrower was set up.

Quick acceptance by the public of institutional lending resulted in changes in private lender practices.

Money is a commodity and the price of money—expressed in interest rates—is determined by the law of supply and demand. When money is in short supply and the demand for it is brisk, interest rates rise. When money is ample and the demand is slight, interest rates decline.

Selection 30: Recalling Facts

1. The opportunities for homeownership were scarce prior to
    ☐ a. 1930.　　　☐ b. 1950.　　　☐ c. 1970.

2. Originally, home mortgages were loans of money for
    ☐ a. two to five years.　☐ b. six to twelve years.　☐ c. fifteen to twenty years.

3. The first organization to stabilize the real estate market was
    ☐ a. the Federal Housing Administration.
    ☐ b. the Veterans' Administration.
    ☐ c. the Homeowners Loan Corporation.

4. When money is in short supply for mortgages, interest rates
    ☐ a. become unstable.　☐ b. increase.　　　☐ c. decrease.

5. FHA mortgage loans are paid in installments every
    ☐ a. week.　　　☐ b. month.　　　☐ c. year.

Selection 30: Understanding Ideas

6. The author feels that most people
    ☐ a. buy only one home.
    ☐ b. know about financing a home but never have the chance to buy one.
    ☐ c. buy and sell several homes during their lifetimes.

7. The author implies that
    ☐ a. banks charge differing rates of interest on mortgages.
    ☐ b. a person must carry life insurance to obtain a bank mortgage.
    ☐ c. most bank mortgages today extend over a period of thirty years.

8. Before the Depression
    ☐ a. banks did not make personal loans.
    ☐ b. mortgages could be obtained easily.
    ☐ c. most banks did not offer money for mortgages.

9. Banks do not loan mortgage money until
    ☐ a. a home has fire insurance.
    ☐ b. a borrower's credit rating has been established.
    ☐ c. a savings account is opened by the borrower.

10. The reader can conclude that
    ☐ a. at one time many people lost their homes to private money lenders.
    ☐ b. bank interest rates are higher than the rates of private lenders.
    ☐ c. real estate appraisals often exaggerate property values.

31. A Green Thumb

Container gardening is especially adapted to contemporary living. Plants in containers are compatible with any decor, be it the straight horizontal and vertical lines of contemporary architecture or the more comfortable lines of the early American home. Plants display great variety of form and texture. They can be used to create instant indoor gardens; they can be moved from one home to another; and they can be moved outdoors in the summer and indoors during the cooler months.

Space is not a problem. Container gardening can be conducted in a single pot on a table or windowsill, in a more elaborate room divider, or in a built-in planter.

Just as there are many kinds of plants, there are many kinds of containers. Plants can be grown in any container that will hold a growing medium. The choice ranges from the common clay pot to cans, jars, boxes, baskets and tubs.

Most people select containers for both their practical and esthetic qualities. These include cost, availability, weight, strength, durability, attractiveness, and decorative and sentimental value.

The size and shape of the container should be consistent with the plant's size and shape. Tall, tapering plants are more attractive in tall, relatively narrow containers. Short, compact plants appear more at home in shallow, wide containers.

Particularly important considerations for good plant growth are the volume and depth of the container, and some provision for drainage. Containers that have drainage holes in the bottom for removal of excess water are best. Watertight containers are difficult to manage; excess water will accumulate at the bottom of the container and injure plant roots by excluding oxygen. Container volume and depth become critical in relation to the quantity of available water and nutrients.

Although the evaporation of water through the container walls is not critical, plants in porous containers will require more frequent watering to maintain moisture levels than will those in nonporous containers.

Besides the right kind of container, some fundamental requirements for plant growth must be provided. Plants need light, water, nutrients, and a satisfactory temperature range.

Light is the most critical requirement. The levels of all the other requirements are adjusted in relation to the amount of light that plants receive. When plants don't have enough light, they grow slowly and become tall and spindly; it becomes difficult to avoid overwatering them. Plants are easier to maintain in good condition when their light requirements are met.

Selection 31: Recalling Facts

1. Tall, tapering plants are most attractive in containers that are
   □ a. long and pointed.   □ b. shallow and round.   □ c. tall and narrow.

2. The most critical requirement for plants is
   □ a. moisture.   □ b. nutrients.   □ c. light.

3. According to the author, some plants
   □ a. can be taken outdoors during warm weather.
   □ b. will produce larger blooms if they are given milk.
   □ c. need water daily.

4. Most flower pots are made of
   □ a. clay.   □ b. fiber glass.   □ c. plastic.

5. Plants in porous containers require extra
   □ a. sunlight.   □ b. warmth.   □ c. water.

Selection 31: Understanding Ideas

6. This article is primarily about
   □ a. caring for indoor plants.
   □ b. growing tropical plants.
   □ c. making containers for plants.

7. Many people believe that tall, spindly plants need
   □ a. extra water.   □ b. more sunlight.   □ c. more nutrients.

8. Porous containers are best suited for
   □ a. cactus plants.   □ b. African violets.   □ c. water lilies.

9. The author implies that
   □ a. ivy is the most popular indoor plant.
   □ b. plants can drown if they are given too much water.
   □ c. most plants should be placed in a northerly window during winter months.

10. We can conclude that
    □ a. vegetables are easier to grow than flowering plants.
    □ b. plants grow indoors with little care.
    □ c. most plants live from three to five years.

32. Secrets of a Volcano

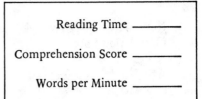
New Mexico Highway 4 climbs westward from the sun-flooded valley of the Rio Grande in northern New Mexico to an elevation of 9,500 feet among blue-green pines in the Sierra De Los Valles. It then drops abruptly into the broad, open grasslands of Valle Grande. Although it is not a well-traveled road because of its remoteness, scientists of the U.S. Geological Survey have traversed the highway numerous times in the 25 years that they have worked in the Jemez Mountains. These scientists are volcanologists who have been unraveling the geological secrets of the Valles caldera, a complex depression some ten miles in diameter. It is an inactive but geologically young volcano that flanks the Rio Grande northwest of Santa Fe.

The Valles caldera doesn't fit the classic picture one usually associates with volcano-barren, lava-covered slopes, matchstick forests felled by fiery avalanches or noxious fumes, and belching of smoke or plumes of steam high in the atmosphere. Actually these phenomena are episodes of Valles caldera's past. Today, the benign volcano is mantled by forests and meadows. The Valle Grande and Valle San Antonio are coursed by sparkling streams of cool, clear water. Cattle graze the banks.

The Geological Survey recognized, prior to World War II, that the Jemez Mountains constituted an ancient volcanic field. Preliminary geologic mapping and sampling further revealed that the youngest episodes of eruption were in the not-too-distant geologic past.

Despite recent volcanic activity, the youngest deposits have been incised by stream erosion, and critical cross-sections of many of its deposits are exposed for study. It was thus seen by Survey geologists as an ideal place for intensive investigations of the workings of a volcano—young enough to retain evidence of almost all its phenomena of activity, but safe from a standpoint of physical hazards. It was ultimately discovered, after painstaking study in the field and laboratory, that the volcano was still cooling off. Rocks of very high temperature still resided deep in its core.

Some of the conclusions reached as a result of the studies by the scientists have changed the science of volcanology. Their investigations are now having a major impact in the development of geothermal energy—a promising new source of power—in the United States. What began as pure research in the esoteric field of igneous petrology has found practical application in a national program of geothermal energy exploration.

Selection 32: Recalling Facts

1. New Mexico Highway 4 reaches an elevation of
   □ a. 4,000 feet. □ b. 9,500 feet. □ c. 12,500 feet.

2. What is the diameter of the Valles caldera?
   □ a. 600 feet □ b. 1,000 yards □ c. 10 miles

3. The slopes of Valles caldera are covered with
   □ a. burned trees. □ b. lava. □ c. meadows.

4. Streams running near the Valles caldera are
   □ a. polluted. □ b. clear. □ c. partially blocked.

5. In geological terms, Valles caldera is
   □ a. an ancient volcano. □ b. an active volcano. □ c. a young volcano.

Selection 32: Understanding Ideas

6. New Mexico Highway 4 is not used by many people because
   □ a. it is dangerously close to the volcano.
   □ b. it is often blocked by rocks and gravel.
   □ c. it is in an unpopulated area.

7. The Valles caldera is located
   □ a. on the Mexican border.
   □ b. in Mexico.
   □ c. in the United States.

8. A geologically young volcano is one that
   □ a. has developed within the past 100 years.
   □ b. has never been studied by geologists.
   □ c. has become inactive in the recent geologic past.

9. The production of geothermal energy requires
   □ a. a moving mass of rock.
   □ b. high temperatures.
   □ c. steam.

10. Originally, the study of Valles caldera was aimed at
    □ a. finding a source of inexpensive electric power.
    □ b. finding a way to predict earthquakes.
    □ c. discovering information about the origins of volcanoes.

33. Sewage Disposal

Municipal sewage is of relatively recent origin as a pollutant. It was first brought to the public attention in the 19th century by a London physician who showed that the city's cholera outbreak had been caused by just one contaminated well. Even though the contamination of drinking water by disease germs has been nearly eliminated in this country, hundreds of communities are still discharging raw sewage into streams and rivers.

When we consider that this sewage contains effluents from toilets, hospitals, laundries, industrial plants, etc., then the potential of the pollutants as a health hazard is apparent.

The problem of municipal sewage disposal is complicated by the fact that, years ago, most cities combined their storm and waste disposal sewers. Many of these combined systems work well, but others cannot cope with sudden heavy rains. When such storms occur, water mixed with sewage may flood and disable treatment plants unless bypassed, untreated, into a stream. In either case, the people may have little protection for several days from these wastes which may contain disease germs.

Even if adequately treated to eliminate the health hazard, sewage is esthetically undesirable because of odors and colors produced. Detergents have posed a particular disposal problem. Although there is no indication that they are injurious to health, they can cause foaming, which can clog treatment plants and, at the least, spoil the scenic beauty of streams.

One consequence of pollution, usually resulting from the discharge of either raw or treated sewage wastes into water sources, is an increase in nutrient levels in these waters. These higher nutrient levels result in a rapid increase in the biological population of the water. Excessive respiration and decomposition of aquatic plants deplete the oxygen content in these waters causing decay which, in turn, may produce an undesirable taste, odor, color, and turbidity. Increasing nutrient contents may also result in an increase in more undesirable species of aquatic life. All these factors make the water unfit for domestic, industrial, and recreational purposes.

Rural and suburban residents should be aware that septic tanks and cesspools are a potential source of pollution to ground water supplies. This is especially true in the suburban areas with a high population density and with no municipal sewage disposal and treatment system available. In some areas, sewage disposal is accomplished by cesspools. Soil research is furnishing guidelines for more effective and safer use of systems such as these.

Selection 33: Recalling Facts

1. Municipal sewage as a pollutant came to public attention in the
   ☐ a. 17th century.   ☐ b. 18th century.   ☐ c. 19th century.

2. A London physician traced the city's cholera outbreak to
   ☐ a. infected rats.   ☐ b. garbage piles.   ☐ c. one well.

3. What has posed a particular disposal problem?
   ☐ a. Detergents   ☐ b. Dyes   ☐ c. Chemicals

4. Nutrient levels in waters where sewage wastes are discharged
   ☐ a. increase.   ☐ b. decrease.   ☐ c. remain unchanged.

5. In the long run, sewage depletes the water's supply of
   ☐ a. algae.   ☐ b. bacteria.   ☐ c. oxygen.

Selection 33: Understanding Ideas

6. In densely populated suburban areas a danger exists from
   ☐ a. streams that do not flow directly to open bodies of water.
   ☐ b. cesspools and septic tanks that contaminate water supplies.
   ☐ c. storm and waste disposal sewers that have been combined.

7. In developing his point, the author makes use of
   ☐ a. scientific arguments.
   ☐ b. convincing testimony.
   ☐ c. common sense observations.

8. This selection is concerned primarily with
   ☐ a. the problems of waste disposal.
   ☐ b. the dangers of drinking unknown water supplies.
   ☐ c. the turbidity of polluted waters.

9. The author mentions the London cholera epidemic
   ☐ a. to prove that the city refused to deal with pollution.
   ☐ b. to prove that medical science once knew little about pollution.
   ☐ c. to introduce the idea of contaminated water supplies.

10. Excessive respiration and decomposition of aquatic plants
    ☐ a. eliminates the concern over municipal water supplies.
    ☐ b. causes an undesirable taste in drinking water.
    ☐ c. allows an increase in the fish population.

34. Low-Pollution Vehicles

Reading Time _____

Comprehension Score _____

Words per Minute _____

The automobile companies believe that the gasoline engine can be made to conform to changing regulations, but with some loss in performance and economy, and at an increased price for the vehicle. There is less certainty that the modified gasoline engine can be made to meet the 1980 goals in an acceptable manner.

A number of alternative power sources has been suggested that could have low emissions. Unfortunately, none of them has been demonstrated to be as simple, economical, flexible, convenient, and acceptable to the motoring public as the present gasoline engine. On the other hand, as the internal combustion engine is made to conform to more stringent exhaust emissions requirements, it is bound to become more complex, more costly and more demanding of maintenance.

The most promising propulsion system for the near future is the gas turbine. It already has been proven acceptable for vehicular propulsion and soon will be applied to production trucks and buses. Expense of production and unresolved technical problems presently limit application to passenger cars. With incentives for and improvements in methods of manufacture, significant cost reductions should be possible. Consumer willingness to pay higher prices for lower pollution could be a major incentive.

Battery-powered vehicles are being built for a variety of uses. Today's technology restricts the choice of batteries to the lead-acid type. This type permits a constant speed range of about forty miles at forty miles per hour. Faster speeds, better acceleration, hill climbing, and stop-and-go operation lower the range disproportionately. Intraurban usage is now possible, but it is likely to take many years before sufficiently improved batteries will be practical for more than limited use. Incentives need to be provided for development of more powerful and lighter batteries, motors, and controls. However, the battery vehicle pollution problem is transferred to the central power station.

There is some indication that a vehicle that combines a system of batteries and a combustion engine, running at constant speed, may be the most promising vehicle from the minimum pollutant standpoint. The development of hybrid propulsion systems should be actively supported.

Other possibilities are fuel cells or alternative fuels, such as natural gas. All of these should be given opportunities for proof of potential. Federal support should be provided for unconventional propulsion system development, including improved batteries, steam engine components, and hybrid systems.

Selection 34: Recalling Facts

1. According to the author, anti-pollution devices
   □ a. decrease cost.   □ b. increase power.   □ c. reduce performance.

2. The author encourages the offering of incentives for the development of
   □ a. lighter batteries.   □ b. rotary engines.   □ c. better exhaust systems.

3. The most promising propulsion system for the future is
   □ a. the solar battery.   □ b. the gas turbine.   □ c. the steam engine.

4. The lead-acid battery permits a speed of
   □ a. 40 miles per hour.   □ b. 80 miles per hour.   □ c. 120 miles per hour.

5. The author discusses the advantages of
   □ a. hybrid systems.   □ b. fuel cells.   □ c. natural gas engines.

Selection 34: Understanding Ideas

6. As the automobile is made to conform to emissions requirements,
   □ a. it demands more maintenance.
   □ b. it requires fewer moving parts.
   □ c. it uses less fuel.

7. Use of the gas turbine in passenger cars will
   □ a. reduce the cost of cars.
   □ b. decrease engine power.
   □ c. significantly reduce pollution.

8. According to the author, the gas turbine engine
   □ a. no longer presents technical problems.
   □ b. is manufactured in several European countries.
   □ c. will be used in trucks before it is used in cars.

9. The author shows strong support for
   □ a. import taxes on foreign cars.
   □ b. government aid in the development of new propulsion systems.
   □ c. legislation to ban the use of gasoline engines.

10. We can conclude that
    □ a. lowering pollution levels is expensive.
    □ b. reducing speed limits lowers pollution levels.
    □ c. future cars will be small in size.

35. A Few City Blocks

Reading Time _____

Comprehension Score _____

Words per Minute _____

Chinatown is a ghetto. Its inhabitants have been unable to participate in the life of the surrounding community. They have been unable to draw upon those community sources of help which have been available to others. It is a ghetto that differs from the ghettos of other racial and cultural groups. The enclosure system in other ghettos has almost invariably been imposed externally. This has been equally true of Chinatown. For the Chinese, however, there have also been strong internal influences which have, until very recently, held the Chinese to the "core" area of Chinatown, an area of a few city blocks. It is estimated that about 37,000 Chinese live in the "core" area of Chinatown. About 60 percent of the city's Chinese population is crowded into one-quarter of a square mile.

The external factors which have kept the Chinese in their ghetto are those usually found in any ghetto situation: protective covenants in other areas of the city, now illegal but still covertly operative, and the general scarcity of low-cost housing which affects all low-level economic groups. Internal factors of language and culture have also acted as barriers to integration. These factors are perhaps far stronger among the Chinese than among other groups, for included in "culture" are the ties of clan and kinship that extend beyond the nuclear family to the clan. The clan includes all persons bearing the same name and families originating in the same district of the homeland. These complex interrelationships involve obligations, responsibilities, and ties based in long, firmly established tradition. Although these interrelations provide a certain aspect of protection, they are by no means exclusively positive for they also involve the imposition of restrictions and hardship.

San Francisco Chinatown is a central and important community for the Chinese population of the United States. It is the headquarters of organizations and associations which exercise considerable control over the lives of the population—over employment for Chinese-speaking workers, over the available housing, and over business and employment. These organizations and associations are internal organisms which operate protective enterprises. They act in a legal capacity for the Chinese-speaking population and, until recently, were the major resource for the immigrant, as well as the old resident in most situations. Those situations involve adjustment to a new country, earning a living, maintaining a family, managing in a world in which virtually every aspect of life is vastly different and largely incomprehensible.

Selection 35: Recalling Facts

1. The author refers to Chinatown as
   □ a. a microcosmic world.
   □ b. a unified community.
   □ c. a ghetto.

2. The population of the "core" area of Chinatown is slightly less than
   □ a. 20,000 people.   □ b. 40,000 people.   □ c. 60,000 people.

3. Most of Chinatown's population lives in
   □ a. one-quarter of a square mile.
   □ b. one square mile.
   □ c. three square miles.

4. The Chinatown discussed in the article is located in
   □ a. Chicago.   □ b. New York City.   □ c. San Francisco.

5. One of the barriers to Chinese integration involves
   □ a. raising a family.   □ b. learning English.   □ c. applying for citizenship.

Selection 35: Understanding Ideas

6. Most ethnic communities are closed off from society
   □ a. by external forces.
   □ b. by internal forces.
   □ c. by a combination of forces.

7. The author implies that the residents of Chinatown
   □ a. live in the poorest community in America.
   □ b. enjoy their clan-centered way of life.
   □ c. are unable to find work in this country.

8. The reader can infer that the residents of Chinatown are
   □ a. depressed.   □ b. oppressed.   □ c. repressed.

9. For many years, organizations in Chinatown
   □ a. have refused to accept federal aid.
   □ b. have provided counseling to emigrants.
   □ c. have helped immigrants adapt to a new country.

10. The reader can conclude that
    □ a. Chinatown is gradually losing its tight structure.
    □ b. Chinatown is expanding to include more city blocks.
    □ c. Chinatown is becoming more representative of middle-class America.

36. Major Risk Factors

Reading Time _____

Comprehension Score _____

Words per Minute _____

More Americans die from heart disease than from any other disease. Every year a million people in this country have heart attacks or die suddenly from coronary heart disease. There are several manifestations of coronary heart disease, all related in part to atherosclerosis, a disease in which fatty materials accumulate in the walls of medium or large arteries.

Cigarette smoking is an important risk factor in the development of coronary heart disease and, by accelerating damage already present as a result of coronary heart disease, may contribute to sudden death. In the total male population, the death rate from coronary heart disease averages 70 percent higher for smokers than for nonsmokers. Men between the ages of 45 and 54 who are heavy smokers have coronary heart disease death rates three times higher than those of nonsmokers. Women smokers in the same age group have coronary heart disease death rates twice those of nonsmoking women.

In addition to cigarette smoking, a number of other biochemical, physiological, and environmental factors have been identified as contributing to the development of coronary heart disease. These risk factors include high blood pressure, high serum cholesterol, overweight, lack of physical activity, and a family history of coronary heart disease. The person who has one or a combination of these factors stands a good chance of developing coronary heart disease. However, high blood pressure, cholesterol, and cigarette smoking are considered to be the major risk factors.

Cigarette smoking acts independently of these risk factors in relation to coronary heart disease, but it can also work jointly with the two major factors to greatly increase the risk of developing this disease. Thus smokers who have hypertension or high serum cholesterol, or both, have substantially higher rates of illness or sudden death from coronary heart disease, while those who are free of these three risk factors have lower rates.

Exactly how cigarette smoking affects the heart is being explored through experimental studies in animals and humans. Nicotine and carbon monoxide, both present in cigarette smoke, appear to be important factors in the mechanism that produces coronary heart disease. Nicotine increases the demand of the heart for oxygen and other nutrients while carbon monoxide decreases the ability of the blood to furnish needed oxygen. Cigarette smoking has other effects on the heart and circulatory system. For instance, both men and women smokers between the ages of 45 and 74 have higher death rates from stroke.

Selection 36: Recalling Facts

1. A major risk factor in coronary heart disease is
   ☐ a. inadequate rest. ☐ b. poor nutrition. ☐ c. high blood pressure.

2. How many Americans suffer from heart failure each year?
   ☐ a. One million ☐ b. Two million ☐ c. Three million

3. Smoking increases the chance of a heart attack by
   ☐ a. 30 percent. ☐ b. 50 percent. ☐ c. 70 percent.

4. Nicotine increases the heart's demand for
   ☐ a. blood. ☐ b. oxygen. ☐ c. exercise.

5. Compared with nonsmokers, middle-aged smokers suffer more from
   ☐ a. pneumonia. ☐ b. bronchitis. ☐ c. strokes.

Selection 36: Understanding Ideas

6. Some doctors feel that a tendency to develop heart disease
   ☐ a. can be detected before birth.
   ☐ b. can be passed on from one generation to another.
   ☐ c. can be disclosed by the color of a person's complexion.

7. The author points out that carbon monoxide
   ☐ a. coats the inner lining of the lungs.
   ☐ b. paralyzes the heart muscle.
   ☐ c. reduces the oxygen-carrying capacity of blood.

8. This article centers on the relationship between heart disease and
   ☐ a. pollution.
   ☐ b. cancer.
   ☐ c. cigarette smoking.

9. Atherosclerosis is characterized by
   ☐ a. a restricted flow of blood to the heart.
   ☐ b. nervousness and insomnia.
   ☐ c. muscle weakness after exercise.

10. A person who has high blood pressure should
    ☐ a. increase his serum cholesterol.
    ☐ b. follow a high protein diet.
    ☐ c. maintain his ideal body weight.

37. Packed Like Sardines

Reading Time _____

Comprehension Score _____

Words per Minute _____

Variation in nature is as enduring a phenomenon as is the rising and setting of the sun. This variation is one of the most difficult problems facing fishery biologists and oceanographers. If the major factors that cause variation are understood, a fishery can be managed to produce the maximum sustainable yield. The ideal is reached if variation is controlled.

In the ocean, this is very difficult with present-day research tools and technology. In inland waters food, spawning, predation, and other conditions that affect the size of a population of fish or shellfish can be controlled more easily.

A striking example of uncontrollable variation is the change in the stocks of Pacific sardine available to fishermen. In 1936, U.S. fishermen took three quarters of a million tons of sardines. In 1967, fishermen were able to take a mere fraction of the peak catch—only about 50 tons. Overfishing was partly responsible. Scientists believe that the changing environment, which affected the capability of the sardine to reproduce and survive, was an important reason for the almost complete disappearance of the species from its former locale.

In the marine fisheries, many fish or shellfish are not caught because markets do not exist for them. Other species are vulnerable to overfishing because the consumer prefers them, and the fish can be caught easily with today's equipment. Fishermen concentrate their effort on these more valuable species. In some cases the fisheries were so intense in the past that production declined seriously. Fishery research has been successful in restoring some of these overfished species, but only because they have been studied and managed.

The halibut fishery in the northeastern Pacific Ocean is a classic example of overfishing, then decreasing catches, and finally restoration of the stocks through research and management.

The International Halibut Commission has conducted research on this giant flounder, the areas in which it is found, conditions under which the species can spawn favorably, and other details of the way in which the fish grows. Every year the Commission, acting on the recommendations of scientists, establishes quotas for the halibut fishing areas. Fishing is discontinued in an area when its catch quota is reached.

The U.S. and Canadian halibut fishery has now been restored, and a catch of 83 million pounds was made in 1966. It is believed that with continuing research and management the catch can be raised even higher.

Selection 37: Recalling Facts

1. The halibut fishery in the northern Pacific is an example of
   □ a. specialization.   □ b. overfishing.   □ c. stock variation.

2. The sardines mentioned in the article are found in the
   □ a. Atlantic Ocean.   □ b. Pacific Ocean.   □ c. Gulf of Mexico.

3. Sardine populations decreased because of
   □ a. changing environment.
   □ b. genetic defects.
   □ c. water pollution.

4. The halibut is described as a type of
   □ a. bass.   □ b. flounder.   □ c. salmon.

5. In 1967 the total sardine catch was approximately
   □ a. 50 tons.   □ b. 400 tons.   □ c. 2,000 tons.

Selection 37: Understanding Ideas

6. In this article the author is most concerned about
   □ a. the establishment of a 200-mile fishing limit for all countries.
   □ b. the control of fish imports from foreign countries.
   □ c. the depletion of certain varieties of marine life.

7. The author feels that some fish populations are declining because of
   □ a. consumer preferences.
   □ b. changing climate.
   □ c. increased interest in sport fishing.

8. To make his point, the author uses
   □ a. an emotional appeal.
   □ b. a factual presentation.
   □ c. biased opinions.

9. The author implies that
   □ a. the populations of freshwater fish are easier to control.
   □ b. most countries are opposed to territorial fishing boundaries.
   □ c. some species of whale are now extinct.

10. "Maximum sustainable yield" is used to mean
    □ a. the greatest amount of fish that may be caught continuously.
    □ b. the restoration of fish stocks in salt water.
    □ c. the decline in production of American fisheries.

38. Ice-cream Plants

Reading Time _____

Comprehension Score _____

Words per Minute _____

One of the insidious things about overpopulation is that its harmful effects are not immediately apparent. To the untrained eye, things may look good at first. There are a lot of animals, and they seem to be in good condition. The real danger signals are subtle and difficult to detect.

The plants that sustain grazing animals have adapted themselves to the periodic loss of some of their foilage. When a grazing animal takes a bite of grass or leaves, the plant has a reserve of energy that enables it to recover and replace the lost foilage in due time. This situation prevails to the benefit of both plants and animals on a balanced range.

But when too many plant eaters dine too often, the animals start to consume the reserves that the plant needs to restore itself. In short, the plant is nibbled to death. The first thing that happens on an overgrazed range is the disappearance of the choice forage plants. These are the plants that the animals like best and eat first. They are sometimes referred to as "ice-cream plants" by range managers. As the ice-cream plants disappear, less palatable plants take their place. To the untrained eye, the range still looks good. It is green and there is vegetation; but to the range manager, who must look at the range through the eyes of the horse, pickings are slim.

After a time the horses start to eat the less palatable plants. As the range continues to deteriorate, the animals are forced to become less choosy about their food. More important, many of the plants they now consume are low in nutritional value. The animals start to show signs of malnutrition, and, as the overgrazing continues, the vegetative cover is depleted to the point that the soil begins eroding.

Yet, even on a severely overgrazed range, it is rare for an animal to lie down to die of simple starvation. Instead, the weakened animals become more susceptible to disease. An infection that healthy animals might throw off may become fatal to the undernourished, and a cold spell or rainy season that would be only a minor inconvenience to healthy animals may decimate a herd weakened by prolonged hunger.

The disaster that has hovered on the horizon for so long may at last strike like lightning, but chances are it will be misinterpreted as something else. The public rarely understands what happens.

Selection 38: Recalling Facts

1. When an animal eats some leaves from a plant, the plant usually
   □ a. dies. □ b. recovers. □ c. wilts.

2. Ice-cream plants are forms of vegetation that
   □ a. grow in cold climates.
   □ b. wilt if they are touched.
   □ c. are preferred by animals.

3. When a range is severely overgrazed, animals often die of
   □ a. disease. □ b. despair. □ c. starvation.

4. Overgrazing is usually caused by
   □ a. drought. □ b. overpopulation. □ c. seasonal migration.

5. An overgrazed range usually looks
   □ a. arid. □ b. barren. □ c. green.

Selection 38: Understanding Ideas

6. The signs of overgrazing
   □ a. are seen first in small animals.
   □ b. are subtle and slow to develop.
   □ c. are apparent only after whole herds have died.

7. The author implies that the range manager
   □ a. is sympathetic towards range animals.
   □ b. is often unaware of overgrazing.
   □ c. is responsible for preventing excessive overgrazing.

8. The less palatable range plants
   □ a. are often poisonous.
   □ b. contain little water.
   □ c. are low in vitamins and minerals.

9. This article is mostly concerned with the effects of overgrazing
   □ a. on cattle. □ b. on deer. □ c. on horses.

10. The author states that most people
    □ a. are not concerned with ecological problems.
    □ b. do not comprehend the dangers of overpopulation.
    □ c. do not care about the survival of wild animals.

39. The Bean Pot

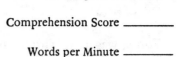

Reading Time _____

Comprehension Score _____

Words per Minute _____

Beans are among the oldest of foods and today are considered an important staple for millions of people.

They once were considered to be worth their weight in gold. The jeweler's "carat" owes its origin to a pea-like bean on the east coast of Africa.

Beans also once figured very prominently in politics. During the age of the Romans, balloting was done with beans. White beans represented a vote of approval and dark beans meant a negative vote. Today, beans still play an active role in politics. Bean soup is a daily "must" in both the Senate and the House dining rooms in the nation's capital.

Beans undergo rather extensive processing before reaching the consumer. They are delivered to huge processing plants where they are cleaned to remove pods, stems, and other debris. Special machines separate debris by weight and then screen the beans by size. Discolored beans are removed by machines equipped with photosensitive electric eyes.

Many varieties of beans may be found on the grocery shelf. Although a shopper will not find all of them, some of the more popular varieties are as follows:

Black beans or black, turtle soup beans are used in thick soups and in Oriental and Mediterranean dishes.

Black-eye peas, also called black-eye beans or "cow peas," are small, oval-shaped, and creamish white with a black spot on one side. They are used primarily as a main-dish vegetable. Black-eye peas are beans. There is no difference in the product, but different names are used in some regions of the country.

Garbanzo beans are known as "chick-peas." These beans are nut-flavored and are commonly pickled in vinegar and oil for salads. They can also be used as a main-dish vegetable in the unpickled form. Similar beans are cranberry and yellow-eye beans.

Great northern beans are larger than pea beans. These beans are used in soups, salads, casserole dishes, and home baked beans.

Kidney beans are large and have a red color and kidney shape. They are popular for chili con carne and add zest to salads and many Mexican dishes.

Lima beans are not widely known as dry beans. Lima beans make an excellent main-dish vegetable and can be used in casseroles. They are broad and flat. Lima beans come in different sizes, but the size does not affect the quality.

Selection 39: Recalling Facts

1. The pea-like bean that inspired the use of "carat" came from
   □ a. Africa. □ b. Asia. □ c. Europe.

2. Voting was done with beans during the age of
   □ a. the Babylonians. □ b. the Greeks. □ c. the Romans.

3. Bean soup is served daily in government dining rooms in
   □ a. Boston. □ b. Memphis. □ c. Washington, D.C.

4. Beans are processed through the use of
   □ a. electric eyes. □ b. pneumatic tubes. □ c. magnetic sensors.

5. Black beans are also known as
   □ a. chick-peas. □ b. kidney beans. □ c. turtle soup beans.

Selection 39: Understanding Ideas

6. Black-eye peas were so-named because
   □ a. they are shaped like eyes.
   □ b. they are blue before they are cooked.
   □ c. they have a black spot on one side.

7. Garbanzo beans are commonly served
   □ a. in thick soups.
   □ b. in salads.
   □ c. in casseroles.

8. Kidney beans are used most often in
   □ a. the spicy dishes of Mexico.
   □ b. the tangy dishes of the Mediterranean region.
   □ c. the aromatic dishes of the Orient.

9. The author implies that great northern beans
   □ a. are preferred by ethnic groups in the United States.
   □ b. are the most versatile of the bean varieties.
   □ c. are often confused with black beans.

10. The reader can conclude that
    □ a. most beans have the same flavor.
    □ b. most beans can be used as main-dish vegetables.
    □ c. most beans grow in warm climates.

40. America's Thirsty Machine

Reading Time _____

Comprehension Score _____

Words per Minute _____

America is the land of the automobile. This country has only 6 percent of the world's population but 46 percent of the world's cars. Right now, there are 97 million privately owned cars consuming 75 billion gallons of gasoline and traveling an estimated 1,000 billion miles a year. The figures also affirm something we know every time we refill our gasoline tank: The automobile is a very thirsty piece of technology. Of the total petroleum supply in the United States, 30 percent goes to quench that thirst. Every year for each passenger car, about 800 gallons of gasoline are consumed.

Other aspects of our commitment to the automobile also bear mentioning here. It takes a great deal of energy to manufacture one automobile—about 150 million BTU's of energy. This is equivalent to 1,200 gallons of gasoline, enough to run a car for about 16,000 miles. We expend energy in the process of shipping cars from factories to showrooms, displaying them for sale and making replacement parts for repairs. One out of six jobs in the nation is associated with the automobile business. About two gallons of gasoline are consumed in the process of making every ten gallons that are pumped into an automobile's gas tank.

Building highways and parking lots has used up much of our land. It has been estimated that we have paved over 21,000 square miles of this country's surface, most of it to accommodate the automobile. The automobile is also the largest contributor to our nation's air pollution problem and a very serious one because most of its pollutants are emitted in our large metropolitan areas. The estimated annual total energy cost of passenger cars in the United States—which includes fuel consumed directly, petroleum refining loss, automobile manufacturing, and retail sales and repairs—is 148 billion gallons of gasoline. Total automotive energy thus consumes 25 percent of gross United States energy.

Aside from the great impact that would occur if everyone seriously practiced conservation, one should stop and think about his own casual use of the automobile. There are numerous situations where better planning and awareness could really make a difference in energy savings and dollars. Because the automobile uses the largest percentage of energy in an average American family's energy budget and almost half of the dollars, the impetus for savings is tremendous.

Selection 40: Recalling Facts

1. What percentage of the world population lives in the U.S.?
   □ a. 6 percent □ b. 13 percent □ c. 18 percent

2. Every passenger car in the U.S. annually consumes
   □ a. 200 gallons of gasoline.
   □ b. 500 gallons of gasoline.
   □ c. 800 gallons of gasoline.

3. The American automobile industry employs one out of every
   □ a. six people. □ b. ten people. □ c. fifteen people.

4. Highways and parking lots in this country total approximately
   □ a. 2,000 square miles. □ b. 10,000 square miles. □ c. 20,000 square miles.

5. What percentage of the gross U.S. energy does the automobile use?
   □ a. 25 percent □ b. 50 percent □ c. 75 percent

Selection 40: Understanding Ideas

6. What portion of the cars in the world are found in the U.S.?
   □ a. One-fourth □ b. One-half □ c. Three-fourths

7. The author implies that
   □ a. Americans waste energy.
   □ b. anti-pollution devices on automobiles are not effective.
   □ c. small cars use energy efficiently.

8. According to the author, most people realize that
   □ a. alternate sources of energy must be found.
   □ b. car pools help to solve some of the energy problem.
   □ c. the automobile uses large amounts of gasoline.

9. Most people do not realize that
   □ a. the manufacture of the automobile requires much energy.
   □ b. gasoline is more expensive than home heating oil.
   □ c. automobile speed lowers energy efficiency.

10. The author suggests that energy savings could be realized
    □ a. with more effective transportation of consumer goods.
    □ b. with better educational programs and planning techniques.
    □ c. with stronger federal controls on energy consumption.

41. Problems of Recycling

Reading Time _____

Comprehension Score _____

Words per Minute _____

Of greatest interest to those concerned with the environmental aspects of solid waste management is the issue of—and the need for—resource recovery and recycling. To many Americans, there is perhaps no greater symbol of our imbalance with nature and our maladaptation to its realities than the fact that we discard millions of tons of wastes every year which do, in fact, have value. The American people realize now that trash need not be mere junk. It has the potential of becoming a significant vein of resources, a mother lode of opportunity for men of vision who can see beyond the horizon.

The American people are right. And those who serve them can no longer view solid waste management solely in terms of collection and disposal. However, something more than the magic of science and technology is required to convert all this waste back into useful resources.

In fact, in proportion to consumption, resource recovery has been steadily losing ground in recent years in virtually every materials sector. Approximately 200 million tons of paper, iron, steel, glass, nonferrous metals, textiles, rubber, and plastics flow through the economy yearly—and materials weighing roughly the same leave the economy again as waste. In spite of neighborhood recycling projects, container recovery depots, paper drives, anti-litter campaigns, local ordinances banning the non-returnable bottle, and the emergence of valuable new technological approaches, only a trickle of the "effluence of affluence" is today being diverted from the municipal waste stream.

The principal obstacles are economic and institutional, not technological. The cost of recovering, processing and transporting wastes is so high that the resulting products simply cannot compete, economically, with virgin materials. Of course, if the true costs of such economic "externalities" as environmental impact associated with virgin materials use were reflected in production costs and if there were no subsidies to virgin materials in the form of depletion allowances and favorable freight rates, the use of secondary materials would become much more attractive. But they are not now. There are no economic or technical events on the horizon, short of governmental intervention, that would indicate a reversal of this trend. If allowed to continue to operate as it does now, the economic system will continue to select virgin raw materials in preference to wastes. This fact should be etched into the awareness of those who look to recycling as a way out of the solid waste management dilemma.

Selection 41: Recalling Facts

1. How many million tons of waste leave the economy yearly?
   □ a. 50 □ b. 100 □ c. 200

2. The principal obstacle to recovering and processing wastes is
   □ a. technological. □ b. ethical. □ c. economic.

3. The favoritism shown to virgin materials can be stopped only by
   □ a. corporations. □ b. industry. □ c. government.

4. Solid wastes can no longer be viewed solely in terms of
   □ a. disposal. □ b. recycling. □ c. recovery.

5. Which one of the following is not mentioned as a solid waste?
   □ a. textiles. □ b. raw sewage. □ c. rubber.

Selection 41: Understanding Ideas

6. This article is primarily concerned with
   □ a. solid waste management.
   □ b. America's new interest in virgin materials.
   □ c. the operation of a recovery plant.

7. The author uses the phrase "effluence of affluence" to symbolize
   □ a. American wastefulness.
   □ b. high purchasing power.
   □ c. declining wealth in America.

8. The author is
   □ a. optimistic about the future of recycled wastes.
   □ b. sarcastic in his attack of the American government.
   □ c. critical of special treatment given to virgin materials.

9. In proportion to consumption, resource recovery in recent years is
   □ a. advancing rapidly.
   □ b. steadily declining.
   □ c. showing very little change.

10. We can conclude that the scientific means for recycling solid waste
    □ a. has not yet been developed.
    □ b. requires further research and testing.
    □ c. is presently available.

42. Trees on Our Streets

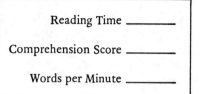

Reading Time _____

Comprehension Score _____

Words per Minute _____

The best trees for any area of the country are those, either native or exotic, which have proved to thrive under the area's prevailing climatic conditions. In wide-ranging species like red maple or red oak, it is best to select from northern populations for cold hardiness.

Trees that are borderline cases are not worth the time and money. For instance, the lovely streets of live oaks in Mobile cannot be duplicated in Washington, D.C., even if seedlings from the northernmost outpost of that species in Virginia are used.

Even when trees have climatic survival potential, however, the variability among seedlings argues against their use in city planting.

We demand much from our city trees. We want uniform and high survival. After all, the young trees planted on our streets cost more than a mature tree of the same species is worth as timber. We want uniform and maximum resistance to pests and to urban stress factors. We usually want uniformity of growth rate and tree form for esthetic reasons. The only way to achieve these goals is clonal selection.

A clone is a group of plants derived asexually from a single individual. The members of a clone are reproduced from the original tree through grafting, budding, or the rooting of cuttings and are all genetically identical. In current horticultural practice selected clones are called "cultivars" and they are given fancy names. The Bradford pear, selected and introduced by the U.S. Department of Agriculture, is an example of a new and useful shade-tree cultivar.

The clone or cultivar thus gives us the maximum in uniformity for desirable characteristics. The clone is also uniform in undesirable traits. If, for example, a well-shaped, fast-growing clone of honeylocust has not been tested and selected for resistance to the mimosa webworm, the steady spread of this introduced insect pest might decimate large-scale plantings of this clone and make chemical spraying the only chance for survival.

There are many cultivars of shade trees currently in the nursery trade—maples, ashes, lindens, and others. But almost without exception, these cultivars have been selected only for their growth and form characteristics. Their resistance or susceptibility to major insect and disease pests is unknown. Their tolerance of urban stress factors such as air pollution and salt is likewise undetermined. The only way to select the best possible trees is through an adequate testing program.

Selection 42: Recalling Facts

1. A clone is produced by
   ☐ a. cross-pollination.   ☐ b. grafting.   ☐ c. root trimming.

2. The Bradford pear is mentioned as an excellent tree for
   ☐ a. color.   ☐ b. fruit.   ☐ c. shade.

3. Honeylocust is often affected by
   ☐ a. worms.   ☐ b. cold temperatures.   ☐ c. leaf wilt.

4. Cultivars are usually selected for their
   ☐ a. shape.   ☐ b. disease resistance.   ☐ c. colorful blossoms.

5. A cultivar that can be purchased in nurseries is
   ☐ a. a maple.   ☐ b. a dogwood.   ☐ c. an elm.

Selection 42: Understanding Ideas

6. The author implies that red oaks
   ☐ a. are common in many areas.
   ☐ b. grow best in warm climates.
   ☐ c. will not grow in the North.

7. According to the author, a cultivar is
   ☐ a. more difficult to breed than a clone.
   ☐ b. less expensive than a clone.
   ☐ c. the same as a clone.

8. In order to produce a clone,
   ☐ a. a male and a female tree must grow near each other.
   ☐ b. a group of trees from one climate must be used.
   ☐ c. only one tree of superior quality is used.

9. According to the article, a clone inherits from the parent tree
   ☐ a. only desirable traits.
   ☐ b. identical traits, good or bad.
   ☐ c. mostly undesirable traits.

10. The reader can infer that
    ☐ a. all forms of oak trees survive well in the North.
    ☐ b. clonal selection is a relatively new method of tree production.
    ☐ c. urban trees are very susceptible to drought.

43. Idaho's Finest

Reading Time _____

Comprehension Score _____

Words per Minute _____

Potatoes are produced in every state, but about half of the commercial crop is grown in Idaho, Maine, California, and Washington.

Most of our year-round supply of fresh potatoes is harvested in September or October. These fall crop potatoes are stored from one to nine months before shipment to retail outlets.

Many potatoes, however, are freshly harvested and marketed from January through September. These are called "new" potatoes. This term is also used to describe freshly dug fall potatoes that are not fully matured.

Most harvesting is done by potato combines that dig the potatoes out of the ground and move them up a conveyor that shakes them, allows soil to drop through, and conveys the potatoes directly into containers or trucks. Usually several workers on the combine pick out any vines, stones, or other debris. A few harvesters also have built-in devices for removing debris.

Potatoes are usually brushed or washed at the packinghouse. Dirty potatoes are unattractive, and the dirt itself contributes weight for which the buyer is paying.

After they are cleaned, potatoes are mechanically sized and are then sorted into grades by packinghouse workers. The potatoes are packed according to grade and size. The grade is often certified during packing by federal or state inspectors.

Over 40 percent of the fresh potatoes are now marketed at retail stores in consumer unit packages. Common types of bags are film, open mesh, paper with mesh or film window, or plain paper. The trend is toward packing so the shopper can see the contents.

Potatoes may be packaged in consumer units at the packinghouse or at wholesale houses in city terminal markets. Retail chains also do a good deal of packing in consumer units in their central warehouses.

Packing is largely mechanized, and bags are generally check-weighed afterwards to ensure that they are slightly overweight and thus allow for shrinkage in marketing.

Red potatoes and some white varieties are sometimes treated with colored or clean wax before shipment to improve their appearance. The Food and Drug Administration requires that potatoes so treated be plainly marked. Under the Federal Food, Drug, and Cosmetic Act, it is illegal to color white potatoes red or to use colored wax to make potatoes appear fresher or of better quality. Several producing states have banned all use of artificial color.

Selection 43: Recalling Facts

1. Potatoes are grown in
   ☐ a. a few states. ☐ b. most states. ☐ c. every state.

2. One of the leading potato states is
   ☐ a. Arkansas. ☐ b. Maine. ☐ c. Michigan.

3. Most of the year-round supply of potatoes is harvested during
   ☐ a. August. ☐ b. October. ☐ c. December.

4. How long are some potatoes stored before shipment to markets?
   ☐ a. Two weeks ☐ b. Six months ☐ c. One year

5. Fall potatoes that are not fully mature are called
   ☐ a. green potatoes. ☐ b. harvest potatoes. ☐ c. new potatoes.

Selection 43: Understanding Ideas

6. The author implies that packers are careful about
   ☐ a. the weight of packaged potatoes.
   ☐ b. the shape of potatoes.
   ☐ c. the wrapper used on packaged potatoes.

7. Most potatoes are purchased by the consumer
   ☐ a. in transparent bags.
   ☐ b. from open bins.
   ☐ c. in plain paper bags.

8. The article suggests that as potatoes age,
   ☐ a. they shed some of their weight.
   ☐ b. they take on a more subtle flavor.
   ☐ c. they become a lighter color.

9. Several potato-producing states
   ☐ a. have required the use of transparent packages for potatoes.
   ☐ b. have banned the use of artificial color in potatoes.
   ☐ c. have outlawed the use of wax on potatoes.

10. The reader can conclude that
    ☐ a. potatoes are least expensive during the winter months.
    ☐ b. potatoes are still dug by hand on most large farms.
    ☐ c. potatoes grow best in cool climates.

44. Twenty-eight Years in a Cave

Reading Time _____

Comprehension Score _____

Words per Minute _____

A special visitor to Guam in early 1973 was greeted at the airport by a cheering crowd of almost four hundred well-wishers, including a representative of the Governor and other business and civic officials. The visitor was not a government official or political dignitary. He had achieved a certain kind of fame, a year earlier, that brought him to the attention of the world.

His name was Shoichi Yokoi. Sergeant Shoichi Yokoi was a straggler of the Japanese Imperial Army and had lived in a cave in Guam for twenty-eight years, unaware that World War II had ended.

And there he was, returning as a tourist to Guam. He was returning as a tourist to a place where he had spent twenty-eight years in hiding! He was given a resounding welcome by the Guamanian populace in testament to the human spirit.

The people of Guam were not surprised to see the former sergeant return. In fact, they have seen their island become a tourist center in recent years, attracting people from all over the world and from Japan in particular. Many of Guam's visitors are former servicemen who participated in the Pacific Theater of Operations in World War II. Others are tourists who see Guam as a tropical paradise that provides all the modern conveniences and luxuries of a contemporary society.

Guam has also become a honeymoon haven for the Japanese, who flock by the thousands to the islands, especially in September and October. In fact Shoichi Yokoi brought his new bride on his return to Guam.

More than 115,000 tourists now visit Guam annually, contributing to the rapidly-expanding economy of the island. The influx of visitors has occasioned a building boom of hotels, restaurants, and other tourist-related services. More than 1,400 first-class hotel rooms now exist on Guam, and a large number of additional rooms are already under construction to accommodate a growing number of visitors. Similar development has been taking place in other facets of the tourist industry, which now is the cornerstone of Guam's private economy.

For years, the people of Guam depended to a large extent on the U.S. military presence on the island. Today, with the encouragement of the federal government, they are becoming more self-sufficient and are diversifying their economy into various fields of the private sector, thereby providing Guam with one of the fastest-growing economies in the Pacific.

Selection 44: Recalling Facts

1. The special visitor to Guam was
   - □ a. a sergeant.
   - □ b. a lieutenant.
   - □ c. a general.

2. Shoichi Yokoi lived in a cave for many years not knowing that
   - □ a. he had been pardoned from prison.
   - □ b. his father had forgiven him.
   - □ c. the war had ended.

3. Most of the tourists who visit Guam come from
   - □ a. Australia.
   - □ b. China.
   - □ c. Japan.

4. Guam is described in the article as
   - □ a. luxurious.
   - □ b. primitive.
   - □ c. quaint.

5. Guam is most crowded during
   - □ a. the summer.
   - □ b. the fall.
   - □ c. the winter.

Selection 44: Understanding Ideas

6. The reader can infer that
   - □ a. the economy of Guam is based largely on tourism.
   - □ b. Guam is an independent British possession.
   - □ c. most people visit Guam because of its beautiful beaches.

7. The standard of living on Guam was improved by
   - □ a. the discovery of oil offshore.
   - □ b. American military presence during the war.
   - □ c. interest in the island as a nuclear test site.

8. The people of Guam are never surprised to see
   - □ a. wealthy Americans coming to the island to live.
   - □ b. people returning to the island for a second or third visit.
   - □ c. foreign companies building factories on the island.

9. The author portrays the people of Guam as
   - □ a. creative.
   - □ b. energetic.
   - □ c. hospitable.

10. In this article, the author
    - □ a. traces the history of Guam to the present.
    - □ b. discusses one facet of Guam's economy.
    - □ c. analyzes the military significance of Guam.

45. A Symbol of the Free Spirit

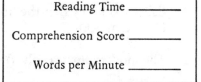

Reading Time _____

Comprehension Score _____

Words per Minute _____

We do not know the tribe of men that first used the horse. Scientists tell us our ancestors were eating horses long before they domesticated them. Historians claim that horses were harnessed before they were ridden.

The horse-drawn chariot dates back to 2000 B.C. in actual records, and there is evidence it had been in use for a thousand years before that.

We also know the modern horse evolved from the dog-sized Eohippus. Its ancestors found their ecological niche on the open grasslands. There they developed the specializations that gave them the speed to outrun their predators and survive.

Fossil remains of the horse and all of his ancestors are common throughout much of North America. For many years, paleontologists believed that the horse first developed here, but later finds on the Euro-Asian continent have now raised questions about this theory. Whatever its origins, we do know that the horse either migrated to or from the Western Hemisphere and eventually became extinct in the New World.

Spanish conquistadors brought the horse back to the Western Hemisphere. In 1519 Cortez landed his troops and his herds of horses at the site of present-day Vera Cruz, Mexico. Coronado's expedition in 1540-41 took the horse to the plains of Kansas. Through the years, some of these Spanish horses escaped or were abandoned, and these became the nucleus of the first wild horse herds in North America.

Between 1519, when Cortez landed in Mexico, and 1803, when Lewis and Clark made their expedition into the West, was a period of 284 years. In the course of history, this is a considerable span of years—ample time to allow the great increase in the number of wild horses that had taken place by the time the pioneers began moving westward in the course of our national expansion.

Western grasslands provided an ideal habitat for the horse and a population explosion occurred. A few horses were captured by the Indians, but this had no significant impact on the wild horse population. By the time English-speaking settlers reached the West, the wild bands were firmly established, and it appeared they had always been a part of the Western scene.

The image of the wild horse running free on the open plains has captured the mind and imagination of modern America and has become a symbol of the free spirit.

Selection 45: Recalling Facts

1. Scientists know that the horse-drawn chariot dates back to
   □ a. A.D. 500. □ b. 1,000 B.C. □ c. 2,000 B.C.

2. The modern horse evolved from an animal about the size of
   □ a. a dog. □ b. an elephant. □ c. a zebra.

3. The horses' ancestors found their ecological niche
   □ a. on plains. □ b. in forests. □ c. near deserts.

4. For many years scientists thought that the horse evolved
   □ a. in Africa. □ b. in North America. □ c. in South America.

5. Cortez brought herds of horses to Mexico during the early
   □ a. 1400s. □ b. 1500s. □ c. 1600s.

Selection 45: Understanding Ideas

6. The West provided an ideal habitat for horses because
   □ a. the weather was temperate.
   □ b. the area was mostly grasslands.
   □ c. larger predatory animals had not reached the West.

7. Horses defended themselves against attack by
   □ a. kicking their hoofs.
   □ b. using their sharp teeth.
   □ c. fleeing at great speed.

8. When Coronado explored the West,
   □ a. he found many herds of wild horses.
   □ b. he captured many wild horses to take home with him.
   □ c. he lost a number of horses that later became wild.

9. The author ends the article with a tone of
   □ a. sorrow. □ b. sympathy. □ c. nostalgia.

10. The author implies that American Indians
    □ a. nearly depleted the wild horse population.
    □ b. captured few wild horses for their own uses.
    □ c. brought most of their horses from Mexico.

46. The Unknown Land

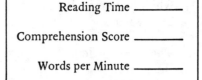

Reading Time _____

Comprehension Score _____

Words per Minute _____

To the seamen of the 18th century who skirted its ice-choked seas in their wooden vessels, Antarctica was known as "Terra Australis Incognito"—the unknown land of the South. Who first saw Antarctic lands is uncertain. On November 17, 1820, Nathaniel Palmer, captain of a Connecticut fur-sealing vessel, almost certainly sighted the continent and in his logbook mentioned seeing land.

On the first official U.S. government expedition to Antarctica in 1838, Navy Lieutenant Charles Wilkes found erratic blocks of continental-type rocks—granite and sandstone. These rocks, carried far northward by floating icebergs, pointed to the existence of a large south polar continent. Today part of Antarctica is called Wilkes Land in his honor.

The pioneering explorations of the continent itself were begun in 1901 by Sir Ernest Shackleton, Captain Robert F. Scott, Roald Amundsen, Sir Douglas Mawson, and many others. Many thrilling stories have been told about this heroic age of Antarctic discovery.

Americans did not become prominent in Antarctic exploration until later. Rear Admiral Byrd was the first to use the airplane, tractor, and radio extensively on the continent, and his expedition in 1928-30 included the first flight over the South Pole. Another American aviator, Lincoln Ellsworth, flew across the continent in 1935 and surveyed from the air the area known as the American Highland.

Expeditions using modern technology inevitably became too expensive for private parties to undertake. The U.S. government officially sponsored the Antarctic Service Expedition to the Antarctic Peninsula and Ross Sea areas in the late 1930s and also the massive aerial photographic mission, Operation Highjump, by the U.S. Navy under Admiral Byrd in 1946-47. These expeditions were followed the next season by Operation Windmill to establish ground control for map compilation and by the Ronne Antarctic Research Expedition in the southern Antarctic Peninsula in 1947. The United States participated in many exploratory and scientific programs carried out during and since the International Geophysical Year of 1957-58.

The continent gradually became a vast experiment in international scientific cooperation. In December 1959, the Antarctic Treaty was signed by twelve countries which agreed to make no territorial claims for the duration of the thirty-year treaty, to use the continent for peaceful purposes only, to open the operations of each country to inspection by any other nation, and to preserve and conserve Antarctic resources.

Selection 46: Recalling Facts

1. When Nathaniel Palmer spotted Antarctica, he was looking for
   ☐ a. whales.   ☐ b. seals.   ☐ c. penguins.

2. The first official U.S. government expedition to Antarctica occurred during the late
   ☐ a. 1830s.   ☐ b. 1860s.   ☐ c. 1890s.

3. How many countries signed the Antarctic Treaty?
   ☐ a. Four   ☐ b. Six   ☐ c. Twelve

4. The first person to use a tractor in Antarctica was
   ☐ a. Amundsen.   ☐ b. Ellsworth.   ☐ c. Byrd.

5. Operation Highjump was concerned with
   ☐ a. climbing mountains. ☐ b. taking photographs. ☐ c. parachuting supplies.

Selection 46: Understanding Ideas

6. The author suggests that Ernest Shackleton and Robert Scott
   ☐ a. discovered Antarctica by accident.
   ☐ b. did not achieve fame in their lifetimes.
   ☐ c. were from European countries.

7. Individual explorations to Antarctica succumbed to government explorations because
   ☐ a. governments were better equipped for research.
   ☐ b. the expense became prohibitive.
   ☐ c. most countries discouraged private explorations.

8. Operation Windmill resulted in
   ☐ a. inexpensive electricity for Antarctic bases.
   ☐ b. a mapping of the Antarctic continent.
   ☐ c. peace agreements between the U.S. and Russia.

9. In Antarctica no country is allowed
   ☐ a. to conduct research on the polar icecap.
   ☐ b. to inspect the operations of other countries.
   ☐ c. to test nuclear devices.

10. We can conclude from this selection that
    ☐ a. Antarctica no longer is considered "Terra Australis Incognito."
    ☐ b. explorations to Antarctica have been halted temporarily.
    ☐ c. Antarctica cannot support life on a year-round basis.

47. Delinquent Youth

Reading Time _____

Comprehension Score _____

Words per Minute _____

A major reason most experts today support concepts such as a youth services bureau is that traditional correctional practices fail to rehabilitate many delinquent youth. It has been estimated that as many as 70 percent of all youth who have been institutionalized are involved in new offenses following their release. Contemporary correctional institutions are usually isolated—geographically and socially—from the communities in which most of their inmates live. In addition, rehabilitative programs in the typical training school and reformatory focus on the individual delinquent rather than the environmental conditions which foster delinquency.

Finally, many institutions do not play an advocacy role on behalf of those committed to their care. They fail to do anything constructive about the back-home conditions—family, school, work—faced by the youthful inmates. As a result, too often institutionalization serves as a barrier to the successful return of former inmates to their communities.

Perhaps the most serious consequence of sending youth to large, centralized institutions, however, is that too frequently they serve as a training ground for criminal careers. The classic example of the adult offender who leaves prison more knowledgeable in the ways of crime than when he entered is no less true of the juvenile committed to a correctional facility. The failures of traditional correctional institutions, then, point to the need for the development of a full range of strategies and treatment techniques as alternatives to incarceration.

Most experts today favor the use of small, decentralized correctional programs located in, or close to, communities where the young offender lives. Half-way houses, all-day probation programs, vocational training and job placement services, remedial education activities, and street-worker programs are among the community-based alternatives available for working with delinquent and potentially delinquent youth.

Over and above all the human factors cited, the case for community-based programs is further strengthened when cost is considered. The most recent figures show that more than $258 million is being spent annually on public institutions for delinquent youth. The average annual operating expenditure for each incarcerated youth is estimated at a little over five thousand dollars, significantly more than the cost of sending a boy or girl to the best private college for the same period of time.

The continuing increase in juvenile delinquency rates only serves to heighten the drastic under-financing, the lack of adequately trained staff, and the severe shortage of manpower that characterize virtually every juvenile correction system.

Selection 47: Recalling Facts

1. According to this author, traditional correctional practices
   ☐ a. have failed. ☐ b. have succeeded. ☐ c. have been ignored.

2. What percentage of youth are involved in new offenses after release from a correctional institution?
   ☐ a. 30 percent ☐ b. 50 percent ☐ c. 70 percent

3. Contemporary correctional institutions are isolated
   ☐ a. politically. ☐ b. economically. ☐ c. geographically.

4. The author calls institutionalization
   ☐ a. a barrier. ☐ b. a crime. ☐ c. a sin.

5. About how much is spent annually on institutions for delinquent youth?
   ☐ a. $250 million ☐ b. $350 million ☐ c. $450 million

Selection 47: Understanding Ideas

6. The author feels that rehabilitative programs should focus on
   ☐ a. the individual delinquent.
   ☐ b. the conditions in which delinquents live.
   ☐ c. the attitudes of the community.

7. The author feels that half-way houses are
   ☐ a. an insult to the intelligence of the criminal.
   ☐ b. a logical solution to the problems of incarceration.
   ☐ c. a danger to the community in which they are established.

8. This article implies that correctional institutions
   ☐ a. are too limited in their treatment.
   ☐ b. extend too far beyond their proposed range.
   ☐ c. are too lax with disciplinary controls.

9. The content of this selection can best be described as
   ☐ a. critical. ☐ b. satirical. ☐ c. narrative.

10. The main idea of this selection is that
    ☐ a. all-day probation programs are less costly than imprisonment.
    ☐ b. adult criminals leave prison with new skills.
    ☐ c. a full range of alternative treatment techniques is needed.

48. NASA and the Computer

Reading Time _____

Comprehension Score _____

Words per Minute _____

Meeting the goals and timetables of the space program demands an extraordinary management effort on the part of NASA and the aerospace industry. It is necessary to marshal the resources of some 20,000 contractors, to coordinate their work, to insure an orderly flow of components to the assembly lines, to build new facilities, to maintain equipment quality and reliability, and to perform a thousand other managerial tasks. It is necessary also to bring in the participation of the scientific community and scores of universities.

Every time a Saturn V rocket is launched, more than 300,000 people in innumerable American factories can view their work with pride. The organizational experience and the broad range of superefficient management techniques, sometimes called the systems approach, constitute a new national resource, already being utilized by other industries and by various levels of government, to promote improved commerce and to attack systematically some of society's most pressing problems.

This social and economic development came about because the engineering management task imposed by the space program is performed in public and without a military objective.

The electronic computer has become one of the most important management tools of business and industry. NASA is helping the advancement toward greater efficiency by making available computer programs at modest cost. Almost every major computer system in the world is made in the United States. In fact, NASA-developed computer programs have proved to be one of the most important fringe benefits from our space program. For example, NASTRAN is an acronym for NASA structural analysis. More than seventy industrial firms, universities, laboratories, and government agencies are now using it to solve their structural engineering problems. This computer management system has been adapted to many applications, ranging from suspension units and steering linkages on automobiles to the design of power plants and skyscrapers. Several more uses are in the planning stage.

NASTRAN is a general-purpose, digital computer program originally conceived to analyze the behavior of elastic structures in the space program. One of its major uses has been in the design of the space shuttle. Since it was first made publicly available in November 1970, hundreds of engineers have become acquainted with its application to industrial management. The computer program is considered virtually indispensable by many structural and design engineers, who estimate that two-thirds of the projects in which it has been applied would not have been attempted without it.

Selection 48: Recalling Facts

1. How many contractors are involved in the space program?
   ☐ a. 20,000   ☐ b. 40,000   ☐ c. 60,000

2. Which rocket does the author mention?
   ☐ a. The Apollo II   ☐ b. The Mercury X   ☐ c. The Saturn V

3. Almost every major computer system in the world is made in
   ☐ a. Japan.   ☐ b. Germany.   ☐ c. America.

4. The NASTRAN computer program has been adapted to
   ☐ a. underwater photography.
   ☐ b. assembly lines.
   ☐ c. suspension units.

5. NASTRAN was made available to the public in
   ☐ a. 1968.   ☐ b. 1970.   ☐ c. 1972.

Selection 48: Understanding Ideas

6. This selection is concerned primarily with
   ☐ a. the design of the NASA computer.
   ☐ b. the goals of the U.S. space program.
   ☐ c. the function of the NASTRAN computer.

7. NASTRAN was conceived originally
   ☐ a. to analyze the elasticity of space materials.
   ☐ b. to develop air-tight containers for solid fuels.
   ☐ c. to predict malfunctions in launch computers.

8. According to the author, the space program
   ☐ a. should be open to public scrutiny.
   ☐ b. is not associated with the Department of Defense.
   ☐ c. has never missed a major launch date.

9. The author seems to be most impressed with
   ☐ a. space achievements.
   ☐ b. equipment reliability.
   ☐ c. project management.

10. We can conclude that NASA
    ☐ a. will manufacture computers in a few years.
    ☐ b. is a diversified operation.
    ☐ c. contributes large sums of money to engineering colleges.

49. Watersheds

Reading Time _____

Comprehension Score _____

Words per Minute _____

Modification of the water yield from a watershed by planned manipulation is a complex process with a potentially great impact on municipal water supplies. The requisite skill is both scientific and artistic; the best practitioners are both highly trained and experienced.

Because of the costs of producing high quality water, and because economic development and a rapidly expanding population will spur the extensions of resource developments into the upper reaches of all watersheds, the approach taken toward the development and use of watershed lands must be both positive and objective. Development programs must be based on the capabilities of the land itself. Federal and state agencies and private enterprise should be supported in their programs for good watershed management to restore the quality of water in all areas.

Where watershed management practices are prudently employed, more clean water can be made available without short-changing other interests. Added benefits of a well-managed watershed include those that accrue from increased opportunities for recreation and land development, soil stability, grazing, and improved wildlife habitat, as well as better forest products.

Most watersheds are more than mere water-producing areas. Except for the extremely rugged, rocky escarpments of major mountain ranges, watershed lands also provide socioeconomic opportunities. Millions of people are attracted to watershed lands every year to enjoy the scenery and facilities for recreation. Watersheds may also provide shelter and sustenance for wildlife and waterfowl. These lands are a source of summer forage for many thousands of our sheep and cattle.

The ideal watershed lands, like water itself, are in a limited supply and are not distributed evenly throughout the nation. Of the 1.9 billion acres of land in the continental United States, many millions of acres have been transformed into cities and towns, farms, airfields, and paved highways. Millions of other acres cannot be classified as water-producing land.

Land management and watershed planning are demanding tasks and often involve the resolution of very complicated patterns of landownership. In most cases, and particularly in the Western United States, the question of water rights rights plays an important, or in some cases a dominant, role. One must consider the wonders of this resource and the effort that has been expended to allow us to use it so easily. While we enjoy our water, we must remember the importance of protecting our water supply. How long could we survive without water?

Selection 49: Recalling Facts

1. How large is the United States land mass?
   □ a. Two billion acres   □ b. Four billion acres   □ c. Six billion acres

2. The question of water rights is particularly important in
   □ a. the South.   □ b. the Northeast.   □ c. the West.

3. People who modify the water yield from watersheds must be
   □ a. patient.   □ b. energetic.   □ c. experienced.

4. Watershed lands are becoming more valuable because of
   □ a. population growth. □ b. foreign trade.   □ c. zoning ordinances.

5. Development of water management areas must be based on
   □ a. state financial resources.
   □ b. land capabilities.
   □ c. public support.

Selection 49: Understanding Ideas

6. The author uses "escarpment" to mean
   □ a. a pool.   □ b. a cliff.   □ c. a dam.

7. Ideal watershed lands
   □ a. are distributed evenly throughout the country.
   □ b. are expanding rapidly in Western states.
   □ c. are not found in some states.

8. According to the article, land that is used for farming
   □ a. is not considered to be water-producing.
   □ b. is more valuable than forest land.
   □ c. is often included in the watershed system.

9. From the article the reader learns that watersheds
   □ a. attract many species of birds.
   □ b. can become contaminated by animals.
   □ c. provide benefits in addition to water supply.

10. The author stresses the need for
    □ a. protecting our water supply.
    □ b. restricting recreational use of reservoirs.
    □ c. finding ways to purify sea water.

50. Wild Horses

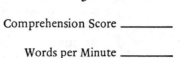

Reading Time _____

Comprehension Score _____

Words per Minute _____

The capture and taming of wild horses has long been a classic theme of American literature.

It is hard to say just when the local ranchers stopped thinking of the wild horse as an asset and started to consider him a pest. The change in attitude was probably tied to many things.

The population of the West had increased, and open land had started to fill up. With the coming of the automobile and the tractor, the value and usefulness of the horse decreased. In some places the wild horse became a serious competitor with domestic livestock for forage. For these and other reasons the rancher's way of looking at the wild horse changed, and between 1920 and 1960 many ranchers would shoot a wild horse on sight.

Then, during this period, another factor was added. The wild horse became an economic asset—but only after it was dead. In an affluent era, more people started to buy canned food for their pets. To meet the demand, enterprising men set up plants to process horseflesh. It became profitable to hunt, capture, and deliver wild horses to the canneries. The wild horse was then the prey of the commercial hunter.

Within a few years, the commercial hunter did what the rancher with his rifle had not been able to do. He seriously depleted the ranks of the wild herds in every state having open range.

The commercial hunter brought modern technology to the business of rounding up wild horses. The wild horse was wily and tough and knew the lay of the land. He could often outrun and outmaneuver a man on horseback, but he was not a match for motor vehicles. The commercial hunter brought in airplanes to flush the animals out of rough country and trucks or pickups to run the animals down once they were in the open. After a horse was roped, a weight was tied to the free end of the lariat, and the animal was left to wear itself out as it dragged the weight and fought the unfamiliar rope. When exhausted, the horse was loaded into a truck and hauled to the processing plant.

Commercial hunters were paid by the pound, and they had to deliver many pounds of flesh to make a living. Few felt that they could afford the extra time required to handle the animals in a humane manner.

Selection 50: Recalling Facts

1. The wild horse became the prey of the commercial hunter for
   ☐ a. its meat.   ☐ b. its hide.   ☐ c. its hair.

2. According to the author, ranchers were never able to control
   ☐ a. horse migrations.   ☐ b. horse populations.   ☐ c. commercial hunting.

3. Horses were rounded up by using
   ☐ a. dogs.   ☐ b. guns.   ☐ c. weights.

4. When horses were taken to the processing plants, they were
   ☐ a. exhausted.   ☐ b. dying.   ☐ c. dead.

5. Commercial hunters were paid by
   ☐ a. the pound.   ☐ b. the horse.   ☐ c. the truckload.

Selection 50: Understanding Ideas

6. Hunters found that wild horses were
   ☐ a. cunning.   ☐ b. fierce.   ☐ c. dangerous.

7. Many hunters felt that
   ☐ a. they were being cruel in their hunting methods.
   ☐ b. processing plants should be outlawed.
   ☐ c. states should not restrict the killing of horses.

8. The author implies that
   ☐ a. hunters were pressured to kill many animals.
   ☐ b. ranchers did not approve of commercial horse hunting.
   ☐ c. horses breed faster than other grazing animals.

9. The year 1920 marks the turning point
   ☐ a. in methods used to capture wild horses.
   ☐ b. in ranchers' attitudes toward wild horses.
   ☐ c. in the condition of grazing lands.

10. The work of the commercial hunter is described as
    ☐ a. an ingenious experiment.
    ☐ b. an unprofitable enterprise.
    ☐ c. a sophisticated operation.

Answer Key

Progress Graph

Pacing Graph

Answer Key

1.	1. b	2. b	3. b	4. a	5. b	6. a	7. b	8. a	9. c	10. c
2.	1. b	2. a	3. a	4. b	5. c	6. c	7. b	8. c	9. c	10. a
3.	1. a	2. b	3. c	4. b	5. a	6. c	7. b	8. b	9. b	10. a
4.	1. a	2. c	3. b	4. b	5. b	6. c	7. b	8. a	9. b	10. a
5.	1. c	2. c	3. c	4. b	5. b	6. b	7. c	8. c	9. a	10. c
6.	1. b	2. c	3. b	4. b	5. a	6. b	7. a	8. b	9. c	10. b
7.	1. c	2. c	3. a	4. b	5. b	6. c	7. a	8. b	9. b	10. a
8.	1. a	2. c	3. a	4. a	5. a	6. a	7. a	8. c	9. b	10. b
9.	1. b	2. c	3. a	4. c	5. c	6. c	7. b	8. a	9. a	10. c
10.	1. c	2. a	3. c	4. a	5. b	6. b	7. c	8. a	9. b	10. a
11.	1. b	2. a	3. c	4. a	5. c	6. a	7. b	8. c	9. a	10. a
12.	1. c	2. c	3. c	4. c	5. c	6. b	7. c	8. b	9. b	10. c
13.	1. a	2. c	3. b	4. b	5. a	6. a	7. c	8. c	9. a	10. b
14.	1. c	2. b	3. a	4. c	5. b	6. a	7. a	8. b	9. a	10. a
15.	1. b	2. c	3. b	4. c	5. c	6. c	7. c	8. c	9. b	10. a
16.	1. c	2. c	3. c	4. c	5. c	6. c	7. b	8. c	9. c	10. a
17.	1. b	2. a	3. a	4. c	5. c	6. a	7. c	8. c	9. a	10. a
18.	1. a	2. c	3. c	4. c	5. a	6. a	7. b	8. b	9. c	10. a
19.	1. c	2. b	3. a	4. b	5. a	6. b	7. c	8. b	9. b	10. c
20.	1. b	2. b	3. a	4. a	5. c	6. c	7. c	8. c	9. a	10. a
21.	1. c	2. b	3. b	4. a	5. a	6. c	7. a	8. c	9. a	10. a
22.	1. c	2. c	3. a	4. b	5. c	6. c	7. c	8. a	9. a	10. b
23.	1. c	2. b	3. b	4. c	5. c	6. c	7. b	8. a	9. b	10. b
24.	1. c	2. a	3. b	4. c	5. b	6. c	7. b	8. a	9. b	10. a
25.	1. a	2. b	3. a	4. b	5. c	6. c	7. c	8. b	9. a	10. b

Answer Key

26.	1. b	2. c	3. a	4. b	5. a	6. c	7. c	8. c	9. a	10. a
27.	1. a	2. a	3. c	4. a	5. c	6. c	7. b	8. b	9. c	10. c
28.	1. b	2. b	3. b	4. a	5. b	6. a	7. c	8. c	9. c	10. b
29.	1. c	2. c	3. b	4. a	5. c	6. c	7. a	8. b	9. a	10. b
30.	1. a	2. a	3. c	4. b	5. b	6. c	7. a	8. c	9. b	10. a
31.	1. c	2. c	3. a	4. a	5. c	6. a	7. a	8. a	9. b	10. b
32.	1. b	2. c	3. c	4. b	5. c	6. c	7. c	8. c	9. b	10. c
33.	1. c	2. c	3. a	4. a	5. c	6. b	7. c	8. a	9. c	10. b
34.	1. c	2. a	3. b	4. a	5. a	6. a	7. c	8. c	9. b	10. a
35.	1. c	2. b	3. a	4. c	5. b	6. a	7. b	8. c	9. c	10. a
36.	1. c	2. a	3. c	4. b	5. c	6. b	7. c	8. c	9. a	10. c
37.	1. b	2. b	3. a	4. b	5. a	6. c	7. a	8. b	9. a	10. a
38.	1. b	2. c	3. a	4. b	5. c	6. b	7. a	8. c	9. c	10. b
39.	1. a	2. c	3. c	4. a	5. c	6. c	7. b	8. a	9. b	10. b
40.	1. a	2. c	3. a	4. c	5. a	6. b	7. a	8. c	9. a	10. b
41.	1. c	2. c	3. c	4. a	5. b	6. a	7. a	8. c	9. b	10. c
42.	1. b	2. c	3. a	4. a	5. a	6. a	7. c	8. c	9. b	10. b
43.	1. c	2. b	3. b	4. b	5. c	6. a	7. b	8. a	9. b	10. c
44.	1. a	2. c	3. c	4. a	5. b	6. a	7. b	8. b	9. c	10. b
45.	1. c	2. a	3. a	4. b	5. b	6. b	7. c	8. c	9. c	10. b
46.	1. b	2. a	3. c	4. c	5. b	6. c	7. b	8. b	9. c	10. a
47.	1. a	2. c	3. c	4. a	5. a	6. b	7. b	8. a	9. a	10. c
48.	1. a	2. c	3. c	4. c	5. b	6. c	7. a	8. b	9. c	10. b
49.	1. a	2. c	3. c	4. a	5. b	6. b	7. c	8. a	9. c	10. a
50.	1. a	2. b	3. c	4. a	5. a	6. a	7. a	8. a	9. b	10. c

Progress Graph (1-25)

Directions: Write your comprehension score in the box under the selection number. Then put an *x* on the line under each box to show your reading time and words-per-minute reading rate.

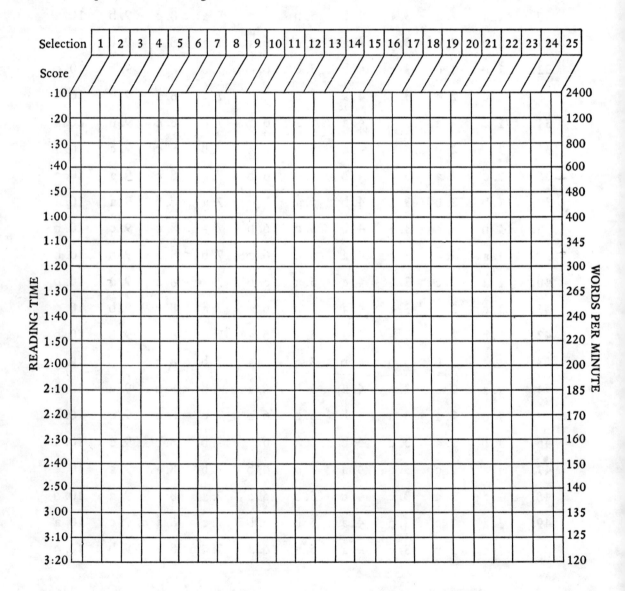

Progress Graph (26-50)

Directions: Write your comprehension score in the box under the selection number. Then put an *x* on the line under each box to show your reading time and words-per-minute reading rate.

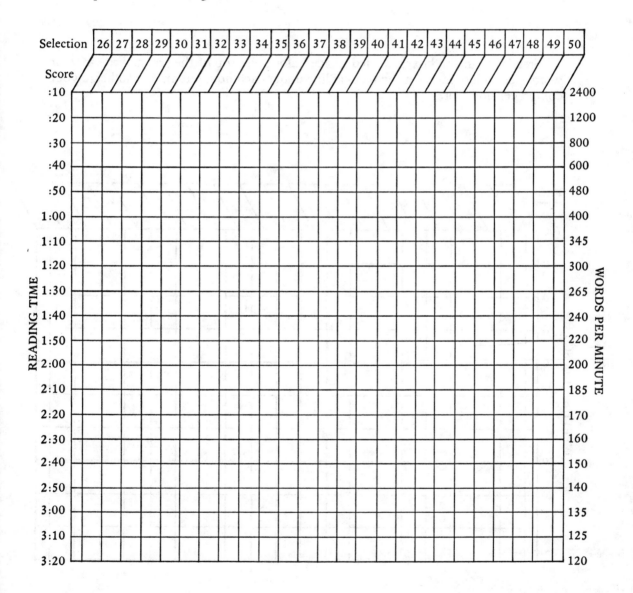

		Selection																							
Score		26	27	28	29	30	31	32	33	34	35	36	37	38	39	40	41	42	43	44	45	46	47	48	49	50

READING TIME — **WORDS PER MINUTE**

Reading Time	Words Per Minute
:10	2400
:20	1200
:30	800
:40	600
:50	480
1:00	400
1:10	345
1:20	300
1:30	265
1:40	240
1:50	220
2:00	200
2:10	185
2:20	170
2:30	160
2:40	150
2:50	140
3:00	135
3:10	125
3:20	120

Pacing Graph

Directions: In the boxes labeled "Pace" along the top of the graph, write in your words-per-minute rate. On the vertical line under each box, put an *x* to indicate your comprehension score.

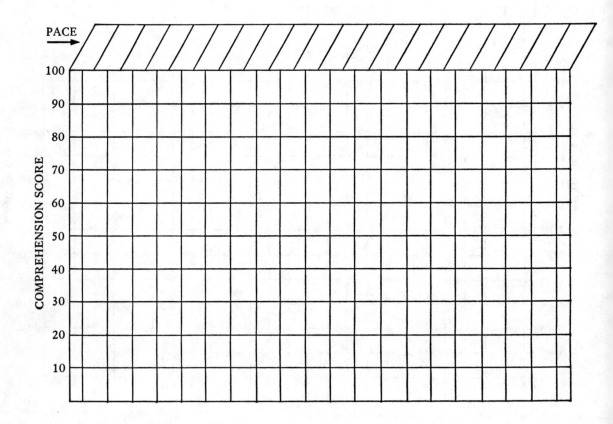